Channel Your
Goddess Energy

This book is dedicated to Elsie Reynolds; a strong and independent spirit with a heart of gold.

Published in 2013 by CICO Books

An imprint of Ryland Peters & Small Ltd

20–21 Jockey's Fields   519 Broadway, 5th Floor

London WC1R 4BW   New York, NY 10012

www.rylandpeters.com

10 9 8 7 6 5 4 3 2 1

Text © Alison Davies 2013

Design and photography © CICO Books 2013

A CIP catalog record for this book is available from the Library of Congress and the British Library.

ISBN: 978 1 78249 072 2

Printed in China

Editor: Marion Paull

Designer: Geoff Borin

Illustrator: Risa Palazzo

For digital editions, visit www.cicobooks.com/apps.php

Channel Your
Goddess Energy

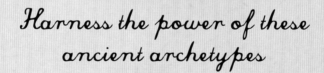

Harness the power of these
ancient archetypes

KIRSTEN RIDDLE

with illustrations by Risa Palazzo

CICO BOOKS
LONDON NEW YORK

Contents

Introduction

The word goddess conjures up a variety of images, from the sultry sirens and sparkling divas of the silver screen to the type of women who ooze charisma and have a certain something that always makes them the center of attention. It's a strong, powerful word that hints at hidden talents and feminine wiles. It's a word that says magic with a capital M, because a goddess is an enchantress first and foremost. She's a heavenly being who can steal your heart with a smile. In the classic sense of the word, a goddess is a female deity, a woman of great beauty, who is admired and adored for her strength and compassion. But in the more mythical sense, she also has powers, strengths, and skills that she can use to help others if she chooses, which, thankfully, in most cases (and legends) she does. For a goddess is usually a generous being, a deity who wants to bestow blessings and help us mere mortals find our way in the world.

Throughout history these beings have existed in our hearts and minds. They've played an important part in spirituality by creating a common bond and a real respect and love between people. Around the world, in every mythology you'll find them taking center stage, inspiring communities and spreading their knowledge. These archetypal figures stay in the subconscious. They speak to our primal instincts, and help us tap into latent abilities and gifts that might otherwise have lain dormant. So it makes sense that we work with them today to manifest the things we want and transform our lives for the better.

There's no hidden secret or key to their magic. It exists all around us, but most importantly it exists in our hearts. When you tap into goddess energy, you're really connecting to that deep innate power in your soul. Like plugging into a wall socket and getting a shot of electricity, you're tuning in to the Earth's energy and your own inner goddess. This book gives you the tools to do just that, to harness your goddess power, by offering a variety of deities and a selection of easy rituals that you can perform, and practices to follow, to connect with them. Risa Palazzo's beautiful illustrations will also help you to connect with these fabulous deities. You may notice that you prefer certain deities to others, that you identify with their struggles or causes. This is perfectly natural; every goddess brings something unique to the picture. Some goddesses are also known by more than one name and alternative names or spellings are placed within brackets.

   As you learn about these fascinating beings from folklore and stories, you'll learn about yourself. By performing the rituals in this book you'll begin to think differently, magically, like a true goddess. You'll notice that people react to you in positive ways, that they hang on your every word. You may even feel yourself hoisted upon a pedestal. But that's fine, because it's all part of being worshipped and adored for the truly unique and magical being that you are.

So go ahead, have fun, and learn how to

be a Goddess!

HOW TO WORK WITH *Your* GODDESS

Working with a goddess is fun and easy. It allows you to be creative and stretch your imagination. You don't have to stick to rigid rituals or follow the suggestions in this book. They are there to provide you with a starting point. The folklore should help you to understand the goddess and the areas that she governs. It's your job to decide how you would like to communicate with her. You can use the given list of associations and make up your own rituals, or use the ones in the book as a guide. Go with your intuition. Experiment and adapt some of the ideas described or come up with your own. Nothing is set in stone and you can't do anything wrong. So be creative and enjoy expressing yourself. Many of the deities in this book are associated with more than one thing; in other words, they may be both a Sun and Moon goddess, or they may be linked to the Air but also have connections with Water. This means that you can be flexible in the way that you work with them.

If in doubt, the best way to form a relationship with a deity is to get to know everything about her. Start by gathering information from books and the Internet. Collect images of the goddess and meditate on them. Read any tales or myths associated with your deity. When you feel you know enough about the goddess you have chosen, you can dedicate an area of your home to her. This doesn't have to be a large space. A shelf or a coffee table in the corner of a room make excellent altars. You don't have to make this a permanent arrangement, either. Think of items that you can add to your table or shelf when you want to work with your goddess. Stones, flowers, plants, candles, and images of animals associated with your deity are all good choices.

You might also want to create a magical worship box for your goddess. You can leave this on your shelf or table and use it to make offerings, or write down personal wishes and requests. The most important thing is to keep looking for new items for your altar. By doing this you are keeping the energy fresh and alive, and promoting a flourishing relationship with the deity.

Another good idea is to set some time aside every week for a mini goddess visualization. Ten to fifteen minutes are sufficient. Treat it as spiritual pampering time. Burn some oil, preferably a scent associated with your deity. Find a comfortable spot and close your eyes. You can use a guided visualization if you like—some excellent ones are available on CD—but it's just as easy to make up your own. Remember, you are in control, this is about you, your power and energy, and your creativity.

The best place to start is to give yourself a portal into the otherworld where you can meet your goddess. Imagine a door, an archway, or even a cave that you can pass through. When you reach the other side, what you see is entirely up to you. Use your imagination. If you like wide open spaces and countryside, then this might be what you see. If, on the other hand, you prefer high mountains , this could be the landscape you choose. It really doesn't matter, as long as you feel comfortable there. Enjoy your surroundings and give yourself time to explore. If you feel ready to meet your goddess, she will appear in some form. But if this doesn't happen, don't worry. Your subconscious mind is in control and knows exactly what you need to see and experience. So just keep repeating the exercise every week and when you are ready, you will meet your deity. Always remember to finish the visualization by returning through the portal you have created.

As you gain more experience and knowledge, you'll find that your goddess comes to you in many ways. You'll start to notice signs and symbols that remind you of her presence as you go about your daily life. Your innate creativity will grow, and you'll feel inspired to follow your heart's desire.

You may feel drawn to different deities, depending on what's happening in your life. This is perfectly natural.

FIND YOUR *Goddess* ARCHETYPE

To give you a helping hand and a starting point, try this quiz, and find out which type of deity you should be working with.

1 Your favorite way to de-stress is to:

- **A** Put on some foot-tapping music and dance the blues away
- **B** Burn some lovely scented oil and meditate
- **C** Spend some time walking outside, appreciating nature
- **D** Have a soothing bath and let the water melt away your anxieties
- **E** Light a candle, close your eyes, and imagine you're in some exotic location

2 In bookshops, you're always drawn to:

- **A** Action and adventure novels
- **B** Spiritual guides
- **C** Natural history books
- **D** Colorful travel guides
- **E** Dark fantasy novels

3 You are most likely to be seen wearing which colors?

- **A** Red, orange, white, silver, and gold
- **B** Yellow, amber, white, and cream
- **C** Green, brown, soft pink, and russet
- **D** Sky blue, turquoise, and light green
- **E** Purple, indigo, and black

4 Choose your favorite stone from this list:

- **A** Amber
- **B** Citrine
- **C** Quartz
- **D** Aquamarine
- **E** Amethyst

5 If you had a superpower, what would it be?

- **A** To throw thunderbolts
- **B** To see into the future
- **C** To heal others
- **D** To fly
- **E** To move objects with your mind

6 What is the most important quality in a prospective partner?

- **A** Passion
- **B** Honesty
- **C** Compassion
- **D** Romance
- **E** Mystery

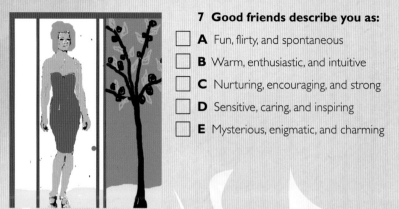

7 Good friends describe you as:

- ☐ **A** Fun, flirty, and spontaneous
- ☐ **B** Warm, enthusiastic, and intuitive
- ☐ **C** Nurturing, encouraging, and strong
- ☐ **D** Sensitive, caring, and inspiring
- ☐ **E** Mysterious, enigmatic, and charming

8 When dealing with a difficult person you:

- ☐ **A** Confront them and get to the heart of the matter
- ☐ **B** Dazzle them with your smile and positive attitude
- ☐ **C** Offer a helping hand, and show your innate resilience
- ☐ **D** Try to understand how they feel and show empathy
- ☐ **E** Tell them what they want to hear, but remain guarded

9 You're thinking of trying a new hobby; which of the following appeals?

- ☐ **A** Rock climbing
- ☐ **B** Astronomy
- ☐ **C** Gardening
- ☐ **D** Scuba diving
- ☐ **E** Magic tricks

RESULTS

Mostly As

You have an affinity with Fire and Ice deities. Like them, you're a passionate soul, who enjoys trying new things. Daring and brave, you're not afraid of a challenge and relish adventure. These resilient goddesses will help you face your fears and move forward into a bright, exciting future.

Mostly Bs

You're most suited to working with Sun and Moon deities. These illuminating beings have a positive attitude, and the ability to remain calm and centered. Like them, you shine your light on others with an enthusiasm that's infectious. Work with these deities to develop your intuitive skills and radiate love.

Mostly Cs

You're drawn to Earth and Creation goddesses. These powerful deities are strong and caring. Like them, you love nature, and appreciate your surroundings. A great communicator, you engage and motivate others. Working with these deities will help you develop compassion and increase your sacred knowledge of the world.

Mostly Ds

You are linked to Sky and Sea deities. Just like them, you're an emotional person, highly sensitive to the needs of others. You give love freely, and enjoy making others feel special. Inspiring and imaginative, you're never short of ideas. These enigmatic deities will help you embrace your talents, and learn to love yourself.

Mostly Es

You have a connection with deities of the Underworld. You're a knowledgeable soul, with an interest in the mysteries of life. Highly creative, just like these deities, you believe in the power of the mind, and enjoy challenging your intellect. Work with these remarkable goddesses to increase wisdom and achieve your dreams.

Earth & Creation

The most inspiring Earth and creation deities are strong, deeply compassionate, and nurturing. They are the mother goddesses, the primordial energy that gives birth to all things. They give of themselves, often sacrificing some part of their being to create something new. At one with their surroundings, they are a part of nature, and the best way to connect with them is to experience the natural world. Get out and about and feel the rhythm of the Earth beneath your feet. Imagine yourself anchored to the roots of the trees, and let that energy support you in all you do. Like the Earth, these deities are stable, and have a steadfast determination, providing peace and comfort in the most trying times. They give love freely, and teach us how to radiate warmth and compassion. Harness their power to develop an affinity with the world around you.

Gaia

PLANET
Earth

STONE
All of Earth's stones

FOOD / DRINK
Grain, oats, potatoes

FLOWER / PLANT
Apple tree

SCENT
Earth, grass, and all herby aromas

ANIMAL TOTEM
All wild animals

MISCELLANEOUS
Soil, grain, foliage, plants

This bountiful Greek goddess of the Earth, a primal being, was considered one of the most powerful deities at the time. She manifested with the sky, the air, and the sea to form the Earth, making her the great mother of all things. She is often pictured as a beautiful young woman emerging from the ground, or clothed in green and surrounded by grain and nature spirits. Gaia (Terra) was born out of chaos. She came into being and created the world. She also created her spouse—Uranus, the sky—from her own body, and is linked to fertility and the cycles of life. Uranus was cruel to Gaia, and made many lusty demands on her. She entreated her son, Cronus, for help. He took a knife and cut away his father's genitals, tossing them into the sea. It's thought that Aphrodite was born from the resulting blood and spray, making Gaia the ultimate creation goddess.

The Ancient Greeks believed that if they petitioned Gaia for help, or asked her to bless an oath, the upshot of the request would be permanent, because Gaia represented the Earth and the Earth is eternal. Gaia is linked to many myths and legends, and is the deity that saved Zeus from being killed by his father, Cronus. She cleverly tricked Cronus into thinking that a stone wrapped in swaddling was his son. Until this point, Cronus had been swallowing his own children in a bid to get rid of them after it was prophesied that one of them would destroy him.

A generous deity by nature, Gaia created the first apple tree, offering it as a wedding present to the Greek goddess Hera.

Gaia can help you to improve any area of your life, and to bring about change. Her message is one of generous giving, of using the talents you've been blessed with to make the world a better place.

GODDESS RITUAL

If you want to change any area of your life, try this simple ritual to Gaia. Hold an apple in both hands and give thanks to the goddess for this nourishing fruit. Cut it in half and scoop out the seeds. Sprinkle them on the soil outside in a pattern of eight, the symbol of eternity. Pour water over the seeds and, as you do this, say: "Gaia, goddess of all creation, help me create the life I want. Let your powers flow through me, to make my life the best it can be!"

Every day make a point of visiting the spot and repeating the chant while visualizing the kind of life you'd like.

GODDESS WISDOM

Gaia is a great goddess to work with if you want to improve your health. Take a potato and begin to peel away the outer layer. Imagine a new healthier you emerging. As you reveal the potato within say: "Out with the old, in with the new, a healthier me for all to see." Use the potato in your cooking, and repeat the chant as you eat.

Demeter

This bountiful Greek Earth goddess governed the harvest and ensured that the land was fertile. Generous in spirit, she served mankind, helping humans cultivate crops and work the land. A truly nurturing goddess, Demeter (Ceres) found it easy to empathize with mortals, and, unlike other deities, who interfered when it suited them, she got involved on a daily basis, and was always on hand to help. Even when the god of the underworld, Hades, abducted her daughter, Persephone, Demeter still found time, in between her constant searching, to help mortals. In one tale she stumbled on an old man gathering firewood. He told her how his son lay dying at home. Demeter was so touched, she took pity on the man and went to visit the boy. On seeing him in his sick bed, she kissed him on the cheek, restoring him to full health with her love and kindness.

Despite her ongoing search, Demeter couldn't find her daughter and, in the end, became so depressed that she withdrew from Mount Olympus, and from her people. The fields grew barren from her lack of attention, and eventually Zeus, king of the gods, intervened and sent Hermes, the messenger god, to persuade Hades to release Persephone.

Demeter was the goddess of agriculture and was often pictured wearing a conical headdress and carrying a sheaf of grain, a torch, and a sacrificial bowl. The Greeks believed she was responsible for the creation of winter, and as such the cycles of life. As a mother goddess, she epitomized unconditional love and the sacrifices that may entail.

PLANET
Earth, Sun

STONE
Carnelian, emerald

FOOD / DRINK
Wheat, bread, honey

FLOWER / PLANT
Sunflower, poppies

SCENT
Orange blossom, cloves, cinnamon

ANIMAL TOTEM
Cat, dog

MISCELLANEOUS
Wheatsheaf, bread, torch

Her message is one of strength and compassion. She shows that it's important to nurture and look after one another, and to be generous of heart and spirit. Work with her to develop a loving heart and mind.

GODDESS RITUAL

To attract wonderful surprises and opportunities into your world, perform this loving ritual. Take a medium-sized pot and fill it half full with earth. Take a handful of your favorite flowering seeds and sprinkle them over the soil. Add a piece of carnelian, and on a piece of paper write the words: "As I nurture the earth, it nurtures me. Good things come my way so easily!" Place the paper in the pot and cover with a generous amount of soil. Spend a few minutes watering the earth while repeating the magical chant. Remember to water the pot regularly, and always give your thanks to Demeter for her help in nurturing your dreams.

GODDESS WISDOM

To radiate love and warmth all day, smother a slice of bread with some honey, eat, and visualize a pink glow surrounding you. Alternatively, you can do the same thing with toast or, if you don't like bread, try breaking up a slice for the birds and passing some love their way.

Cybele

This Roman Earth goddess is connected to caves and the dark places beneath the ground, which is why the color black is associated with her. Originally called Phrygian, she was goddess of caverns and wild things. As Cybele, she became an Earth Mother, associated with fertility not only in women, but also in the soil. She is the deity who governs wild animals, in particular bees. The Romans dedicated a special celebration to this goddess, Cybele's festival of joy, which was a decadent affair with much merriment—a time for music, dancing, and plenty of drinking. Offerings were made in the form of sacrifices, which were often bloody and gory. Her followers went to extremes to show their devotion, in particular men. Some would castrate themselves and dress up as women to emulate the Earth Mother.

In many pictures, Cybele wears a crown that resembles city walls and features turrets and a gate; this is because she ruled over fortresses and other high places, such as mountains and cliffs. A goddess of nature, she was deeply in love with the god of vegetation, Attis. In one Greek version of the tale, Attis is a mortal man, who steals Cybele's heart. She pursues him, despite the fact that he loves another, and in the end he kills himself. The spot where his blood flowed on the ground is where the first violets sprang forth. In another legend, Cybele's love for Attis sends him mad and he kills himself, but Jupiter resurrects him as a pine tree.

PLANET
Earth, Mars

STONE
Jet, onyx

FOOD / DRINK
Nuts, pomegranate seeds, wine

FLOWER / PLANT
Pine tree, violet

SCENT
Fresh pine, violet

ANIMAL TOTEM
Lion, hawk, leopard

MISCELLANEOUS
Gate, key, mountain, tree, turret, cave, soil

This vibrant goddess is often pictured with lions or leopards at her feet—a sign of her immense power and the fact that she had total control of all the wild things that roamed the Earth.

Cybele's message is one of joy and celebration. She warns of taking things to the extreme, but also shows us the importance of being able to laugh at ourselves. In tune with the feral nature of Earth, Cybele helps us bend and flow with the twists and turns of life.

GODDESS RITUAL

Attract more love and happiness into your life by performing this ritual to Cybele. Gather together a handful of seeds—pomegranate and sunflower are both good choices. Stand outside and sprinkle them in a large circle on the ground. Stand in the center of the circle, and skip from one foot to the other, increasing the speed of each hop. Turn this into an Earth dance by spinning around and throwing your arms in the air. Have fun and enjoy acting the fool. After a few minutes, stop, breathe deeply, and imagine you are rooted to the Earth by the soles of your feet. Say: "Cybele connects me to the Earth, to the joy within, and to the energy of the world."

GODDESS WISDOM

If you want to get close to Cybele, and learn how to go with the flow, climb a mountain or hill. Stand at the top with your arms outstretched and say: "I am free, I am powerful, I am loved."

"Cybele connects me to the Earth, to the joy within, and to the energy of the world."

Athena

PLANET
Venus, Jupiter

STONE
Red calcite

FOOD / DRINK
Olives, wine

FLOWER / PLANT
Olive tree

SCENT
Cedar, sage

ANIMAL TOTEM
Owl, snake

MISCELLANEOUS
Trumpet, flute, pot, shield, spear

The wondrous Greek Earth goddess Athena (Minerva) sprung forth from Zeus's forehead, fully formed and dressed in armor. Always Zeus's favorite child, she was one of the few deities who was allowed to use his thunderbolts. A goddess of war, intellect, wisdom, the arts, and agriculture, Athena governed many areas, and was seen as something of a super-deity. A fierce protector of the realm, Athena fought in wars, mostly to defend her people and the kingdom. An ingenious inventor, she created the bridle so that horses could be tamed, and also the plough and the yoke, so that they could be used to work the fields. This is why she is closely linked to agriculture, and handicrafts. She also invented the trumpet and the flute, making her a much-loved deity of music and the arts.

The half-sister of Hercules, Athena had a generous spirit, and befriended many heroes in Greek mythology, such as Jason and Perseus. She carried a goatskin shield and an aegis, which had a fringe of snakes. When Perseus killed Medusa, the snake-headed gorgon who, with a glance, could turn med to stone, he gave her head to Athena so that she could add it to her aegis. Athena's rival to become patron of the city of Athens was the god of the sea, Poseidon. She had to prove her merit and used her magic to make an olive tree spring forth on the citadel as an offering to the people. Poseidon tried to outdo her by using his trident to bring forth water, but as the sea was salty, the people were not impressed, and preferred Athena's gift. As a result, she is often associated with olives and olive oil.

Athena's message is one of reason. Although she was a fearless warrior, she preferred to think her way out of trouble, using her intellect to outwit opponents. She teaches us to rely on our intuition, to broaden our knowledge, and to take a step outside of our comfort zone.

GODDESS RITUAL

To increase intellect and get you firing on all cylinders first thing in the morning, try this easy ritual to Athena. Take a handful of fresh sage leaves and steep them in a bowl of hot water. Lean over the bowl and, with a towel over your head, breathe deeply. Inhale the cleansing aroma. Imagine it traveling around your body, cleansing your aura and your soul. Relax and enjoy the vibrant scent. Finally, ask Athena to bless you with her strength and vitality throughout the day.

GODDESS WISDOM

To get close to this awe-inspiring goddess, use olive oil in your cooking. You can also combine a little olive oil with essential oils and massage into your skin. As you do this, picture yourself glowing with power.

Izanami

PLANET
Earth

STONE
Quartz crystal, any precious jewel

FOOD / DRINK
Water

FLOWER / PLANT
Lotus, iris

SCENT
Floral fragrances

ANIMAL TOTEM
Fish

MISCELLANEOUS
Love, marriage, mountain, star, spear, sea

This heavenly goddess descended from the sky with her husband Izanagi. When they reached Earth, they built a palace for themselves on the newly formed land. In Japanese folklore, they're considered to be the first couple. They created the ritual of marriage, and were associated with fertility and childbirth.

Their first-born child, Leech, was deformed, supposedly because Izanami had spoken out of turn during the marriage ceremony. Not one to be deterred, Izanami decided to hold the ritual again, this time with Izanagi speaking first. After this, she gave birth to many children. Her first few babies became Japanese islands, and, following this, came a string of deities who governed the wind and the mountains, making her a true creation goddess. Unfortunately, her mothering qualities were to prove fatal when she gave birth to Kagutsuchi, a Fire god, who burned her to death. It's at this point that she descended into the underworld, or Yomi as the Japanese called it. Here she became a living corpse.

Izanagi, desperate to see his wife again, traveled into the depths of the underworld to entreat her to come back to the land of the living with him. Izanami said she would need to seek approval from the other gods, but in the meantime she implored him not to look at her. Izanagi ignored his wife's pleas. He broke off a tooth from his comb and lit it. He was horrified to discover his wife's decomposing body, and fled in fear. Izanami, not too impressed by her husband's disobedience and his reaction to her less than perfect state, sent a

horde of demon hags after him. Some might say the moral of this tale is that hell hath no fury like a woman scorned but Izanami was deeply hurt by her husband's response, and being an emotional deity, lashed out with passion. Inevitably, she stayed in the underworld and allowed her husband to return to the land of the living, releasing him from their marriage vows.

Izanami teaches us to relinquish control of the events in our life, to loosen our grasp on the things we desire. In doing so, we become free, and able to give and receive love unconditionally. A passionate deity, her message is one of respect and tolerance.

GODDESS RITUAL

Fulfill your dreams and manifest your wishes by climbing a mountain for Izanami. You don't have to go for anything too strenuous; a short climb up a hill is sufficient and will have the same results. With each step, imagine you're getting closer to your goal. When you reach the top, take a deep breath and shout your wish out loud, while imagining how you'll feel when you attain it. You might want to throw something into the air as an offering, such as a flower, or a piece of earth. Feel the release of letting go of your intentions, and be confident that the universe and Izanami are listening and working their magic.

GODDESS WISDOM

Izanami is a creation goddess with attitude. If you want to make your mark on the world, write down your goal, and keep the paper in a purse together with a quartz-crystal spear. Imagine the crystal sending light to your wish every day.

Atira

This powerful goddess is sacred to Native Americans. Often referred to as Mother Earth, she is linked to fertility and creation, and is the basis of all things. She is also associated with corn, which is a symbol of her abundance and her ability to feed and nurture the people. Atira is worshipped in a special ceremony, known as Hako, which involves painting an ear of corn blue to represent the sky, and attaching white feathers to it to represent clouds. Atira is often associated with stars. The Pawnee people, who held Atira in high regard, believed that the first man and woman were created from the morning and evening star.

Wife of the dominant creator god Tirawa, Atira governed the wild places, in particular the fields and the forest. Although she is associated with corn and the growing of crops and was married to the god of agriculture, her people were more concerned with hunting. They felt this was a respectful way to honor the goddess. They believed that she provided all the things they needed upon the Earth to survive. Mother of every living creature, she was respected for her caring nature.

Atira had a daughter, Uti Hiata, who, like her mother, cared deeply for her people. She taught them how to make tools and grow food from the land.

Atira is the supreme mother goddess and represents the environment today. She is in all things, the ground that we walk upon and the air that we breathe. Work with her if you want to

PLANET
Earth

STONE
Any of Earth's stones

FOOD / DRINK
Corn, grain, wheat, barley

FLOWER / PLANT
Corn

SCENT
Sandalwood, lavender

ANIMAL TOTEM
All wild animals and living things

MISCELLANEOUS
Soil, feathers, corn, pebbles, rocks

connect with nature and feel inspired. Her lesson is to be at one with the Earth, to respect every living thing, and to look after the environment.

GODDESS RITUAL

Get close to Mother Nature and feel energized by the Earth with this simple ritual. Take off your shoes and stand barefoot outside. Feel the earth beneath your feet and imagine that, as you stand, tiny threads of light stretch from your soles, connecting you to the roots below. Imagine you are anchored to Earth. Stretch your arms above your head and reach for the stars. Say: "Mother Earth, your nurturing energy flows through me. I am supported by you, and I stand tall." Jump up and down on the spot.
Feel Earth supporting you, and feel the energy flood every part of your body.

GODDESS WISDOM

Pay homage to Atira by taking care of every living creature. Simple things, such as feeding the birds in your garden, or offering to help out at an animal shelter, will help you connect with her power and radiate love. Take an interest in your surroundings, and get out and about in nature as often as you can.

"Mother Earth, your nurturing energy flows through me. I am supported by you, and I stand tall."

Ix Chel

PLANET
Moon

STONE
Carnelian, jasper, agate

FOOD / DRINK
Water

FLOWER / PLANT
All herbs

SCENT
Frankincense, myrrh, patchouli

ANIMAL TOTEM
Snake, rabbit, jaguar

MISCELLANEOUS
Rivers, lakes, crescent Moon

This Mayan goddess of creation and the Moon was also called Lady Rainbow and associated with the sky. She was responsible for sending rain to nourish the crops. The rain was thought to spring from her sacred womb and, because of this, she is also a fertility goddess. She would sit in the heavens, a being of light, with the ability to glow in all the colors of the rainbow. She captivated many of the other gods, but she had eyes for just one, the Sun god, Kinich Ahau. She tried desperately to win his admiration, but in doing so neglected her duties on Earth, causing terrible storms and floods. In the end, it wasn't her stunning looks that won him over, but her weaving skills. She bore the Sun god four sons, who became the jaguar gods. They were named after the cardinal points and responsible for holding up the four corners of the sky. But the love affair had no happy ending. Kinich Ahau was an abusive god, and Ix Chel soon tired of his behavior. One night she crept away, taking the form of the jaguar so that she could move quickly and unseen. She left him and went to live on a sacred island many miles away. There she spent her days helping the other women weave and also assisting them in childbirth.

Ix Chel is often pictured as a serpent crone, carrying a water vessel, or with a serpent on her head. This is because snakes are associated with medicine and wisdom, and Ix Chel was known for her healing powers. She is also portrayed holding a rabbit in her hands, to symbolize fertility and the cycles of life. The Mayan people believed that she was responsible for determining the sex of a baby in the womb, and that if they worshipped her, she would bless their unborn child and help it grow.

Work with this goddess when you want to inspire new growth in any area of your life. Her message is one of determination, of going up against the odds and of holding true to your beliefs. Ix Chel teaches us to keep going when times are tough.

GODDESS RITUAL

To get things moving on the love front, or to invite new opportunities into your life, try this ritual. Add a couple of drops of frankincense and patchouli essential oils to a tablespoon of sunflower oil. Massage into a white candle while thinking about your request. Light the candle and say: "Ix Chel, with your power strong, help to make my life move on. Bring in the good, the love, the light, from this moment, on this night." Let the candle burn down and relax in the knowledge that positive changes are on the way.

Kwan Yin

This generous and tender-hearted Chinese goddess is often referred to as the mother of all Buddhas. Extremely caring, it was thought that Kwan Yin, or Kuan Yin, as she is sometimes called, could hear the cries of the world, and took that suffering upon herself in an attempt to ease all pain. She is often compared to the Virgin Mary.

A mother goddess, she is nurturing and warm, and tries to help anyone in need. She is particularly associated with children and childbirth, and many altars were created to petition her for help when conceiving a child. Often shown with cupped hands to represent the womb, she is also pictured holding the pearls of illumination in one hand, as a symbol of her sound judgment and compassion, and a small vase containing "sweet dew" in the other. This concoction was believed to be the nectar of wisdom and understanding, which she would pour upon Earth, so that everyone could experience true peace. She has strong links with the sea, and is often pictured riding the waves on a lotus flower, and sometimes on the back of a water dragon. She is the goddess of sailors and fishermen, offering protection and strength while they are at sea.

One of the most famous stories associated with the goddess is that she was a Buddhist, who, having shown great mercy and sacrifice during her life, was offered the chance to enter nirvana upon death. But as she stood at the gates to the otherworld, she heard cries of great anguish from Earth, and could not bring herself

PLANET
Earth

STONE
Pearl, jade

FOOD / DRINK
Water, rice

FLOWER / PLANT
Willow tree, lotus

SCENT
Sandalwood

ANIMAL TOTEM
Dove

MISCELLANEOUS
Dragon, scroll, pearls, vase, sea

to leave its people. This is why she has a reputation for tenderness and empathy.

Kwan Yin's message is one of unconditional love and compassion. She teaches us to treat others as we would wish to be treated, to show respect, and to offer a helping hand to those in need.

GODDESS RITUAL

To develop a compassionate spirit and to attract more love into your life, follow Kwan Yin's lead. Take a scroll of paper and write down all the things for which you are thankful. Think of all the blessings in your life, and make a note of them. When you are ready, roll up the paper, and tie it with some white string or ribbon. Place it in a wooden box with a piece of jade. Sprinkle a few drops of sandalwood on the paper, and say: "I am a loving, giving being of light, I give thanks for the blessings in my life."

Return to the scroll when you need to remind yourself of all the love in your life, and continue to add to the list as you receive more blessings.

GODDESS WISDOM
To radiate love and light, act like Kwan Yin. Extend a helping hand to others, and carry out acts of kindness every day. This doesn't have to be anything big—a smile, or a compliment, is enough to brighten someone's world and spread the love.

"I am a loving, giving being of light, I give thanks for the blessings in my life."

Inanna

Often called queen of the heavens because she was linked to the foundation of all things, Inanna is a Sumerian goddess of love, fertility, and creation. Named the Giver of Life and linked to sexual energy and passion, Inanna was thought to have used all this energy and drive to form the universe. Known for her healing powers, she is also the keeper of all emotions, ranging from love and joy to fear and anger. A clever deity, she outwitted the god Enki in order to give her people the gifts of wisdom and inspiration. Inanna was highly respected and became the queen of seven temples across the Sumer. The Babylonians also knew her as Ishtar.

According to legend, she descended twice, coming from heaven to Earth to rule her people, and then traveling from Earth to the underworld to visit her sister, Ereshkigal. The reasons for her visit vary. In some tales, she wanted to steal the leadership of the underworld from her sister. To reach Ereshkigal she had to leave all her worldly possessions, including her jewels, at the entrance to the otherworld and travel through seven different gates. When she found her sister, Ereshkigal showed no mercy, and hung Inanna on a peg to die. On hearing of Inanna's descent and death, Enki sent two creatures to rescue her body. The creatures showed Ereshkigal understanding, and she allowed them to take Inanna's corpse and bring her back to life. Although this sounds like a macabre story, both Inanna and Ereshkigal learned great lessons from the experience. Inanna became vulnerable to the cycles of life and death, and Ereshkigal learned compassion.

PLANET
Venus, Earth

STONE
Lapis lazuli

FOOD / DRINK
Water

FLOWER / PLANT
Rose

SCENT
Musk, jasmine, patchouli

ANIMAL TOTEM
Lion

MISCELLANEOUS
The number 7, rosette, star, knot

INANNA

Inanna's message is one of knowledge and learning. She wants to experience more of the world, learn about the underworld, and pass on her wisdom and inspiration to the people. She urges us to be open to new experiences. By exposing ourselves to new circumstances, we become stronger and more confident.

GODDESS RITUAL

Liberate yourself and open your heart to love with the help of the goddess Inanna. Invest in some rosewater, and spray yourself liberally with it, from head to toe, after washing. Take a piece of red thread or cotton and tie seven knots in it. As you do this, think about the seven gates that Inanna passed through, and how each one brought her closer to freedom. Say: "Inanna, hear my plea above, help me find my way to love. Free my spirit and my soul, help me reach my heart's true goal." Carry the knotted thread with you as a charm to increase your personal power and allure.

GODDESS WISDOM
Experiment with scents to tap into the sensual power and energy of this goddess. Take half a cup of almond oil and add a couple of drops of patchouli and jasmine essential oils. You could also add rose or vanilla extracts. Mix the oils and massage the liquid into your body, while imagining yourself adored like a goddess.

"Inanna, hear my plea above, help me find my way to love. Free my spirit and my soul, help me reach my heart's true goal."

Tara

PLANET
Earth

STONE
Rose quartz

FOOD / DRINK
Fresh water, anything sweet

FLOWER / PLANT
Lotus flower

SCENT
Rose

ANIMAL TOTEM
Owl, raven

MISCELLANEOUS
The colors white and green,
stars, the third eye

This enigmatic Hindu mother goddess is the creator of all things. One of the oldest deities, her name in Sanskrit means "star" and also "she who brings forth life." Tara appears in two forms—her compassionate, peaceful nature is embodied as White Tara, and her bold, protective side as Green Tara. In Buddhism, Tara is seen as the female Buddha and is often called the Enlightened One. Thanks to her all-consuming power, she can take many forms, appearing as other deities in mythologies around the world. She is believed to be at one with every living thing, and like the Buddha, she is wise, spiritual, and loving.

In Tibet there are many legends about this goddess. In one, she is born from a lotus blossom floating on the lake. This blossom was formed from the compassionate tears of Avalokitesvara, the original bodhisattva, who was reincarnated as the Dalai Lama. He was so distressed by the state of the world, and the pain that he experienced, that he started to cry. His tears brought forth Tara, the female version of his goodness. Tales say she was granted the right to change her human form to that of a man, but Tara preferred her female body. Her priority was the welfare of her people and being able to care for them.

In her guise as Green Tara, the goddess showed her fiercely protective nature. During the Chinese army's occupation of Tibet, refugees spoke of seeing visions of Green Tara and described how she helped and guided them to safety.

Today you can work with Tara to overcome problems and help you through stressful situations. You can call upon her benevolent nature, and ask her to soothe your soul. Her lesson is one of inner peace, and cleansing the spirit.

GODDESS RITUAL

To ask for Tara's help with any difficult situation, make an altar to the goddess. Cover a coffee table with either a green or white tablecloth. Add a bowl of fresh water, a piece of rose quartz, a vase of white roses, and any images that you feel are appropriate. Sit before the altar, and ask for Tara's blessing. Say: "Sweet Tara, bless me with your love, bring divine assistance from above, to turn around my current plight and move forward into the light." Spend some time sitting peacefully before the altar every day.

Sea & Sky

Some of the most enigmatic and enchanting goddesses are deities of the sea and sky. They will help you learn how to love yourself. Governed by their emotions, these beings follow their heart in all things. They know the beauty and healing power of love, and how to use it to make the world a better place. Sensual and inspiring, they have empathy with the mortal world, and will often involve themselves in human affairs, in an attempt to soothe pain and ease problems. They bring hope, optimism, and a delightful sense of fun. Like the sky and the sea, they are tempestuous and changeable. Connect to them by breathing deeply and using by water to cleanse your body and soul. These deities challenge you to be true to yourself at all times. Flexibility is important to these beings, and they will show you how to go with the flow and embrace the ups and downs of life.

Nut

PLANET
Moon, Sun

STONE
Sodalite

FOOD / DRINK
Water

FLOWER / PLANT
Sycamore tree

SCENT
Lavender

ANIMAL TOTEM
Cow, pig

MISCELLANEOUS
Stars, the color blue, water pot
or jug, the number 5

This beautiful Egyptian sky goddess was known for her incredible kindness and compassion. Her deep-blue skin covered in stars gave Nut a striking appearance, which attracted a lot of attention. Although she married the Earth god Geb, who was also her brother, some tales claim she had an affair with the god of words, Thoth. When Ra found out that she was married to her brother, he was furious, and fearing what kind of children they would produce, laid down a curse that she could never give birth on any day in the calendar However, Nut was already pregnant, and she was distraught at the thought of never becoming a mother. She enlisted the help of Thoth, who challenged the Moon to a gambling game and, eventually, after many months of playing, Thoth won five extra days of light. During this time Nut gave birth to her children, including the god Osiris and the goddess Isis, who later became lovers. This is how Nut became known as Mother of the Gods. The extra five days were used every year to honor and worship her strength and generosity.

As a sky deity, Nut is often pictured stretching in an arch across the sky, with only her fingertips and toes touching the ground. If storms raged through the land, it was said that Nut had slipped a little closer to Earth. Considered to be mother of both the Sun and the Moon, she sometimes took the form of a great cow, with eyes that shone like the stars. She is also pictured as a giant sow, suckling her young, another reference to her power as a goddess of creation, and a mother.

A water carrier, Nut appears in pictures and carvings balancing a pot of water on her head, and to enhance this image, the hieroglyph of her name is a water pot.

If you want to excel and reach your goal in life, Nut is the goddess with whom to work. She teaches perseverance and determination. She shows us that we can all shine like the stars, if we're prepared to work hard, develop a resilient spirit, and have faith.

GODDESS RITUAL

Shine with natural beauty and confidence by performing this water ritual in the evening. Take a bowl of warm water and add five drops of lavender essential oil. If you're feeling brave, stand under a shower and pour the water over your head; otherwise, splash the water over your face and neck. As you do this, imagine that a veil of twinkling stars covers you. Finish by saying: "Great mother goddess Nut, shower me in starlight, help me sparkle clear and bright, from this moment, on this night."

GODDESS WISDOM

To get close to Nut's power, and achieve your dreams, make a point of standing beneath the stars every night. Imagine you have a magical lasso in your hands and that, as you throw it, you hook a star. Take a deep breath and say: "I reach for the stars at all times!"

Iris

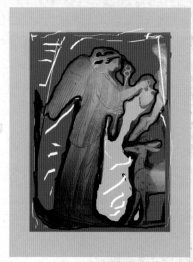

This stunning Greek goddess of the rainbow also ruled the sky and the sea. She was a messenger goddess, running errands for the other deities, and was often referred to as Hera's personal handmaiden. Her father was Thaumas "the Wondrous," a marine god, and her mother was Elektra "the amber," a cloud nymph. Her name means rainbow, and in its other form, Eiris, means messenger. Iris is depicted as a young woman wearing a multicolored gown that shines like the rainbow. She has two beautiful golden wings and a herald's rod, and is often shown holding a pitcher of water. In pictures, she stands between Hera and Zeus, serving them nectar from a golden jug.

Iris was responsible for replenishing the rain clouds with water from the sea—it had been noted that rainbows often spanned the coastal line, and appeared to dip into the ocean. There are also tales of her taking water to the other gods in times of trouble.

Iris, unlike many of her Greek counterparts, had the ability to travel to the underworld. She was responsible for keeping the peace, and for restoring balance and harmony after a storm. Faithful and loyal, Iris inherited all the goodness in her family—her sisters were the cruel and vengeful Harpies. Although she was a great beauty, she remained a virgin goddess. Her main role was always to serve others, and to run errands to and from the underworld.

Iris teaches us to be humble, to help and look after others, and to show love in our actions. Her message is one of hope and loyalty.

PLANET
Sun

STONE
Jasper

FOOD / DRINK
Water, mead

FLOWER / PLANT
Iris, lemongrass

SCENT
Iris, rose, lemon

ANIMAL TOTEM
Dove

MISCELLANEOUS
Bright colors of the rainbow,
water, wings, letters

She demonstrates that true beauty comes from the heart, and that real happiness comes when we give love and go that extra mile for someone.

GODDESS RITUAL

To attract good fortune and inspiration into your life, try this simple Iris ritual. Add a drop of rose and lemon essential oils to a bowl of water. Leave on a window ledge, to catch the light of the sun for a few minutes. Stand in the shower and tip the water over your head. As it falls, imagine that you are standing in the light of a colorful rainbow. Say: "Iris may your colors flow, let them make my spirit glow. Lady fortune bring to me, happiness and joy times three!" If you don't want to get soaking wet, you can perform a mini version of this ritual by using the infused water as a hair rinse, or dipping your hands into the liquid.

GODDESS WISDOM

To lift your spirits and rejuvenate your soul, introduce bright colors into your wardrobe. Add a splash of red by wearing a bright scarf, or red lipstick, and experiment with a range of shades in your accessories. Imagine your aura shining in all the colors of the rainbow, and watch as heads turn.

Hathor

Often called Queen of the Sky, and the Mother Goddess, Hathor is the vibrant Egyptian deity of the arts, music, and dance. She was invoked to inspire artists and writers, and there are many tales of her using her creative talents, in particular her dancing skills, to cheer up the Sun God, Ra. A nurturing deity, the cow is her sacred animal because of its mothering instincts, and Hathor is often depicted with cow's horns and a sun disk upon her head. Sometimes she even appears as the Celestial Cow, a constellation of stars that supports the heavens above and provides the backdrop of the sky. She is associated with the All-Seeing Eye, and also the ankh, a symbol used to attract good fortune. Revered by the pharoahs, Hathor also appealed to many women of the royal family, who would take on the title "Priestess of Hathor" as a mark of respect to the goddess.

A keen protector of women, Hathor governed pregnancy and childbirth. She was also a fertility goddess and linked to the river Nile. She offered protection for those who traveled to the underworld after death, and because of this she is often linked to the sycamore tree, the sacred tree of the dead. The sycamore was believed to offer shade and refreshment to those taking the long journey from this life to the next.

Hathor is sometimes associated with the mirror. This is because the handheld mirrors of the Ancient Egyptians were crafted from bronze or copper, and the handles were often shaped in the form of the goddess or the ankh, one of her sacred symbols.

PLANET
Sun

STONE
Emerald, turquoise

FOOD / DRINK
Water

FLOWER / PLANT
Sycamore tree, rose

SCENT
Rose, sandalwood

ANIMAL TOTEM
Cow, swan, dove, lynx

MISCELLANEOUS
Ankh, sun, lamp, music and dancing, mirror

Hathor's message is one of encouragement and enthusiasm. She teaches us to have a go, and unleash our hidden talents. She shows us that there is no need to be afraid. By working with her, we can draw the strength and courage that we need to follow our dreams.

GODDESS RITUAL

To improve self-esteem, and feel good inside and out, try this simple ritual to Hathor. Take some rosewater and spray it liberally on a handkerchief. Place lightly over your face and breathe in the sweet aroma. Imagine that you're a flower coming into bloom, stretching upward to the Sun. Say: "I am a being of light and love. I am blessed with joy from up above." Finally, spray the rosewater lightly over your clothes and hair, and picture a cloak of roses covering your shoulders as you go about your business.

GODDESS WISDOM

If you're in need of a boost, or you just want to unleash your creative spirit, then sing. Hathor loved music and singing, and the louder the better. Pick a song, learn it word for word, and sing at the top of your voice. Pretend you're a superstar. Enjoy those feelings of adulation and let your hair down.

"I am a being of light and love. I am blessed with joy from up above."

Aphrodite

PLANET
Venus

STONE
Rose quartz

FOOD / DRINK
Apple, strawberry

FLOWER / PLANT
Rose, oak trees

SCENT
Apple

ANIMAL TOTEM
Dove

MISCELLANEOUS
Handheld mirror, shells,
pearls, the sea

One of the most famous deities of love and beauty, the Greek goddess Aphrodite (Venus) was born from the foam of the sea. Many images show her riding to the shore in a giant scallop shell, and shells of any kind are often associated with her. Married to the craftsman god Hephaestus, she lived on Mount Olympus, but her distance from the Earth did not stop her interfering in the lives of mortals. She was thought to be the cause of the Trojan War, after bribing Paris, a mere mortal, with the love of Helen, the wife of the king of Sparta, so that he would award her the Golden Apple, a prize for the fairest goddess. This angered the king, and was said to be the start of all the problems.

Aphrodite was a powerful deity and like many goddesses she wore a magic girdle, which increased her powers. A pleasure-seeking goddess, Aphrodite adored the good things in life, and had a deeply indulgent streak. She delighted in good food, wine, and the adulation of others. Despite being married, she had a deep passion for Ares, the god of war, with whom she had a secret love affair. Known for her extreme fits of jealousy, she even attempted to thwart her own son's happiness with the beautiful mortal Psyche, but in the end, true love could not be denied and they were married.

Said to inspire lust and admiration in deities, mortals, and beasts, Aphrodite's power was legendary. A symbol of erotic love and sensuality, she was never alone, and had many illicit liaisons, but far from feeling guilty about her affairs, Aphrodite reveled in every union. She truly believed in the power of love, and knew that the key to matters of the heart lay in self-love.

Today she teaches us to be thankful for the blessings in our life and to celebrate the good things. Most importantly, she advocates learning to love ourselves, for it is from self-love that all other aspects of love grow.

GODDESS RITUAL

If you're looking for love, or you just want to deepen an existing love bond, this ritual to Aphrodite will help. Take a shell and a handheld mirror, both objects linked to this goddess. Hold the mirror and gaze at your reflection. Imagine your face glowing with light. Say: "As I see, so it shall be, an inner beauty radiates from me." Next, whisper your love request to the shell and finish by asking for Aphrodite's blessing. Do this every Friday evening while the moon is waxing (getting bigger.) Friday is the day most associated with this deity, and the waxing moon helps to draw your wishes closer.

GODDESS WISDOM
Rose quartz will link you to this goddess. Place over your heart, breathe deeply, and imagine a ball of pink light hovering over your chest. Make a wish for love and send it out to the universe by blowing a kiss.

Arianrhod

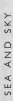

PLANET
Moon

STONE
Moonstone

FOOD / DRINK
Wheat

FLOWER / PLANT
Ivy, birch tree

SCENT
Jasmine

ANIMAL TOTEM
Owl, white sow, spider

MISCELLANEOUS
Silver wheel, stars, cauldron,
silver coins

This benevolent Welsh goddess of the sky and Moon is often referred to as the Goddess of the Silver Wheel. A beautiful silver-clothed goddess and lady of the stars, she was thought to descend from the heavens in a white chariot so that she could be close to the sea below. Daughter of the Moon goddess Don, she is the ruler of a magical, heavenly realm, the Caer Sidi, where souls can rest, and which is said to be the fount of all inspiration for poets and artists. Linked to death and re-incarnation, Arianrhod would carry the souls of those who had passed away to the land of the dead, also known as Emania, transporting them on her mighty wheel. She is Protector of the Dead and of those souls awaiting reincarnation.

A triple goddess, Arianrhod represents the three phases of womanhood—Mother, Maiden, and Crone—but is most often associated with the mothering aspect. She is linked to the Moon because the Celts believed that this was a symbol for the womb. Gifted with the power to shapeshift, her creature of choice was the owl, and she would often transform into a giant owl to fly through the night. She had the power to see into the darkest places, including the subconscious mind. Like the owl, she was considered wise, knowledgeable, and extremely intuitive, able to sense injustice and shed light upon any area. A goddess of mystics and magicians, Arianrhod is a powerful ally in any kind of magical work. Her special day is December 2, when festivities take place to worship her, and to give thanks for the starry heavens above.

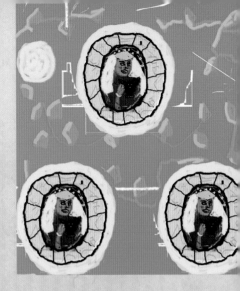

Arianrhod's message is one of clarity and justice, of seeing beyond the veil and trusting your instincts. She teaches us to look beyond the surface, to recognize the signs and symbols of the subconscious mind, and to work with them to improve understanding of ourselves and the world around us.

GODDESS RITUAL

To improve your intuitive skills and connect to your higher self, try this ritual to Arianrhod. On the night of a full Moon, take a pot or a cauldron and a handful of silver coins. Stand outside and place the pot at your feet. Throw the coins into the pot, while chanting: "Moon bright upon this night, Arianrhod bless me with second sight. Wisdom be mine, from this moment in time, my higher self reveals true wealth."

Carry the pot inside and leave it in a prominent place. Every night repeat the chant and make an offering to the cauldron. This can be a silver coin, a stone, an image of the Moon, or a sprig of ivy. Any of the items associated with the goddess will help to manifest your wishes.

ARIANRHOD

Oshun

This Yoruban goddess of love and beauty is also linked to fresh water and often appears near rivers, ponds, and waterfalls. She is described as an alluring young woman, and sometimes appears as a mermaid. Known for healing the sick and helping the poor, she has a generous nurturing spirit and is linked to fertility. She governs the River Oshun, and is especially revered in riverside towns. Dance is an important part of this goddess's worship, and she will often take over a devotee's body during the festivities. If this happens, the follower is said to be blessed, and given a new name to mark her out as special.

Mother of all birds and fish, Oshun was married to the storm god, Shango. A sweet-natured deity, she had a love of luxury, and enjoyed the sensual pleasures of life, including good food, music, and dance. She also loved to eat sweet things, including honey, which is often left as an offering to her. Whoever leaves this gift must always taste the honey first. This is a mark of respect to the goddess, to show that the honey is not poisoned in any way.

In addition to her nurturing powers, Oshun was a powerful mystic, able to read the future using cowry shells. She was taught this skill by the first gods and, eager to help her people, she passed it on, together with the knowledge associated with divination.

Today Oshun can help with all matters of the heart. With her psychic powers, she can reveal the future, and a way forward. She will help you get in touch with your intuitive side and embrace the

PLANET
Moon

STONE
Aquamarine, amber

FOOD / DRINK
Honey, pumpkin, oranges, wine

FLOWER / PLANT
Orange blossom

SCENT
Ylang Ylang, patchouli, rose, orange

ANIMAL TOTEM
Peacock, vulture

MISCELLANEOUS
Shells, waterfalls, music, dance,
the number 5

ebb and flow of life. Oshun's message is one of intuition, of learning to read signs and symbols, and of trusting your emotions in all things.

GODDESS RITUAL

If you're looking for love, and want to open your heart to the universe, try this easy ritual to Oshun. First thing in the morning, take a tablespoon of honey and add it to a glass of hot water. As you stir, ask Oshun to bless you with love and help you embrace the day ahead. Drink while picturing yourself covered by a shower of golden light. Also think about the goodness of the water replenishing and cleansing your system. If you prefer, you can pour this mixture over your head in the shower, to unleash your natural beauty and give your skin a glow.

GODDESS WISDOM

To tap into Oshun's vibrant power, and enhance your innate beauty, decorate your home with peacock feathers or patterns. Choose fabrics, curtains, and throws that incorporate the image and colors of this bird, and mix with shades of gold to add that extra magical touch of opulence.

Marici

In Buddhist mythology, Marici is the goddess of the dawn, associated with the first rays of light in the sky. A formidable character, she is often seen riding through the sky on seven pigs, and sometimes she appears with three heads, one of which is a sow. In Tibet, many shrines are dedicated to the goddess, and devotees regularly invoke her at dawn with requests for protection and strength. She is associated with war, death, and military action, and her appearance can be scary, as she has multiple, terrifying heads, each adorned with jewelry made from human skulls. However, she is also often pictured as a beautiful young woman, sitting peacefully and meditating on a lotus flower.

Marici has a great deal of power and is in charge of a range of celestial and earthly deities, who govern both blessings and punishments. The lotus flower forms the basis of her sky chariot in which she flies into the path of the Sun's rays, making her almost invisible. In many images she is depicted as having red or gold skin.

Sometimes referred to as the Diamond Sow, Marici was popular with the Samurai, who believed that worshipping this goddess would help them transcend into the spiritual realm. They thought that if they could tap into Marici's power, they would become invincible, because they were no longer concerned with matters of life and death.

Today we can use her power to give us strength in our convictions. Marici, the guardian of life and light, can help us find our

PLANET
Sun

STONE
Diamond, quartz crystal

FOOD / DRINK
Saffron

FLOWER / PLANT
Lotus

SCENT
Rosemary

ANIMAL TOTEM
Pig, boar

MISCELLANEOUS
Weapons, light, dawn, the colors red, gold, and white

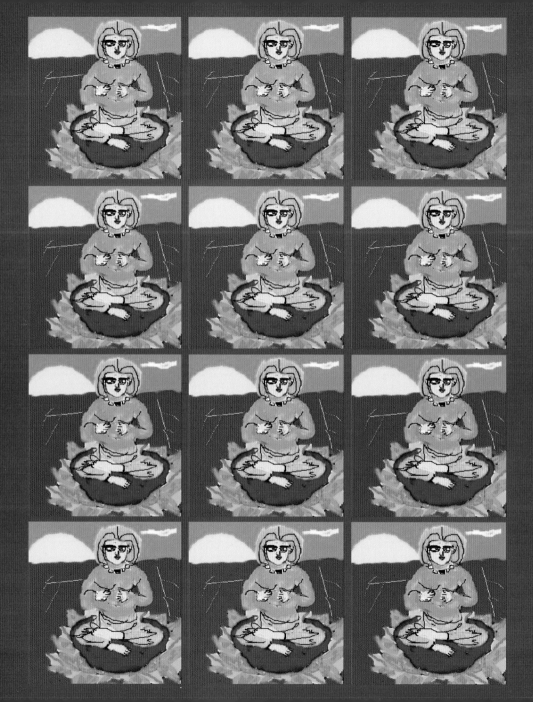

voice, face our fears, and overcome any obstacle. Marici's message is one of finding inner peace, from which all strength comes.

GODDESS RITUAL

Follow the Tibetan path of worshipping this deity at dawn, when she is at her most powerful. Light a red candle and burn some rosemary-scented oil. Look to the sky and make a wish for protection and strength. Imagine a fiery circle of light surrounding you. Say: "Marici, with your power strong, protect me as the day goes on. Bless me with an inner peace, so any negativity can be released." To enhance those feelings of ability and confidence, carry something red or gold with you, such as a keyring, scarf, or piece of jewelry.

GODDESS WISDOM

To tap into Marici's passion and strength, incorporate color into your life. Red, gold, and white are her shades, so dedicate a corner of your home to the goddess, and decorate it with candles, objects, pillows, and throws in these colors. When you need strength and confidence, sit and meditate in this area.

"Marici, with your power strong,
protect me as the day goes on.
Bless me with an inner peace,
so any negativity can be released."

Coventina

This Celtic goddess of springs, wells, and rivers also governed the cycles of life, and is associated with the underworld. In Scotland, she was often referred to as the Goddess of Featherless Flying Creatures who could pass into the otherworld, and so is associated with prophecy and divination. The Celts would throw coins and other objects into the wells and springs they dedicated to Coventina, and ask for her blessing. They believed that these wells were the belly of the earth, and as such represented the womb. This meant that Coventina was often associated with fertility and childbirth. A nurturing deity, she had healing powers, and people would bathe in her waters, and drink from them, in the hope that it would soothe their ailments.

She is often pictured as a water nymph, floating on a leaf on the river and carrying a pot of water. She is linked to the ebb and flow of time and was worshipped as a triple goddess, which meant she could appear as Mother, Maiden, or Crone. Her favorite guise was as the Maiden and many plaques and carvings have been found depicting her as a youthful beauty. Her links to the otherworld gave her faerie connections and some believe she was a queen of the faerie realm, in addition to being queen of all the river deities.

Cups, cauldrons, pots, and wells are all associated with this goddess and used in magical rituals to petition her help. Working with Coventina will ensure that you gain a deeper insight into the cycles of life. She will show you that your cup is overflowing with joy,

PLANET
Moon

STONE
Pearl

FOOD / DRINK
Water

FLOWER / PLANT
Hibiscus, pine

SCENT
Pine

ANIMAL TOTEM
Fish, kingfisher

MISCELLANEOUS
Cup, cauldron, well, spring, leaves, coins, water, pins

and how to appreciate both the good times and the bad. Her message is one of renewal, of cleansing the spirit, and of going with the flow.

GODDESS WISDOM

To refresh your spirit, and your vigour for life, make a cup of tea and drink to the goddess. If tea isn't your thing, just boil some hot water, let it cool a little, and add a squeeze of lemon and a spoonful of honey. As you sip, give thanks for the nourishing properties of the water.

GODDESS RITUAL

Move closer to your goals and improve your energy levels by performing this ritual to Coventina. Take a large pot and leave it outside to gather rainwater. You can add a small bowl of tap water to the pot if necessary. Every day, throw a coin or a pin in the pot and say: "Coventina, refresh my soul, help me move closer to my goal. Shine your healing light on me, so that a brighter future I can see." When the pot is full, remove any offerings and use the water to feed your plants and flowers. Then start the process again.

Thetis

The sensual Greek goddess Thetis is one of the Nereids, the fifty daughters of Nereus and Doris, who lived in the Mediterranean Sea. These beautiful creatures were always on hand to help sailors and those in trouble, emerging from the waters as enchanting nymphs.

Thetis was a beauty, and greatly admired by Zeus. He was desperate to make her his wife, but soon changed his mind when he heard the prediction that her first-born would overthrow his own father. Instead, Zeus gave Thetis to a mortal man, Peleus. She bore him a son, the famous Achilles, whom she tried to make immortal. One of the many tales about how she did this suggests that she covered his tiny body in ambrosia and then placed him on the fire to burn away all the mortal parts. In another, more popular tale, she dangled him by the ankle in the river Styx, in the hope that the river's magical waters would make him invincible. The problem with her theory was that the waters had to touch every part of his body. As she held him by his heel, this never touched the water and so remained vulnerable. In the end, being wounded in this weak spot caused his death during the Trojan War.

Thetis had the gift of prophecy, and could also change shape at will. Like the waters she inhabited, she could easily merge with the sea, and appear in many different guises. When Peleus first tried to charm her, she transformed into fire, water, a lion, and a serpent in a bid to escape him. A pleasure-loving goddess, Thetis is often linked to music, dance, and activity. She is also thought to be a fertility goddess, because the sea gives life to many creatures.

PLANET
Neptune

STONE
Aquamarine, quartz

FOOD / DRINK
Salt, water

FLOWER / PLANT
Apple tree, gold and yellow flowers

SCENT
Geranium

ANIMAL TOTEM
Lion, serpent, fish, dolphin

MISCELLANEOUS
Fire, water, salt water, driftwood, sand

GODDESS WISDOM

Make your bathroom a sacred shrine to Thetis, and use it as a peaceful retreat to recharge your batteries. Invest in images of the sea and beach, and include blue and white candles. Burn geranium-scented oil, and place clusters of aquamarine and quartz around your bath.

Thetis teaches us to be fluid like the sea in which she lives. Her lesson is one of pleasure and movement, of being flexible in all things, and of adapting to the changes life brings. She eases anxiety and can help us cope with stressful situations.

GODDESS RITUAL

To ease anxiety and develop inner confidence, try this ritual to Thetis. Sprinkle a handful of sea salt in a dish of water. Take a piece of quartz crystal and place it in the water. Say: "Thetis, as your power flows, so my strength and confidence grows."

Leave the crystal over night, and remove it in the morning. Put it in a small bag or velvet pouch that you can carry with you, together with a pinch of salt and a couple of apple seeds. This charm will ease worry and stress, and help you remain focused and firing on all cylinders.

THETIS

65

Yemoja

This African goddess of the ocean is also a mother goddess, and patron of all pregnant women. Deeply nurturing, she represents the maternal aspect of divinity. She gave birth to the Yoruba tribe with whom she traveled all over the world when they were taken as slaves to different countries. Through these travels, she is also worshipped in Brazil and linked to the Virgin Mary.

Originally a water deity, Yemoja (or Yemaya) was called Mother of the Children of Fish. Images often depict this goddess as a beautiful mermaid. Appearing out of nowhere, she is considered to be the Queen of the Ocean, because of her capacity to help fishermen and those lost at sea. Her followers wear necklaces of blue beads and quartz crystal, and pregnant women are often given turquoise jewelry as a symbol that Yemoja is looking out for them.

Since she gave birth to both fresh and salt water, she is known as Mama Watta. Tales tell that after being subjected to horrific violence, she flung herself from the top of a mountain, down to earth. Her stomach split during the fall to reveal the first man and woman, and the blood that flowed created all the rivers and the seas. Throughout the world she is honored on different days, but September 8 is usually the day most associated with her power.

Her message is one of strength and determination. Despite any wrongdoings, Yemoja continued to thrive and help her people. She teaches us to rise up against adversity and to develop a tenacious spirit. There is also a sense of fun about this goddess, and as the

PLANET
Moon, Neptune

STONE
Turquoise, quartz, pearl

FOOD / DRINK
Watermelon, water

FLOWER / PLANT
Seaweed, white and blue flowers

SCENT
Orange, lemon, raspberry

ANIMAL TOTEM
Fish, dolphin

MISCELLANEOUS
Turquoise, coral, shells, blue beads, anchor, rattle, key

playful mermaid, she encourages us to be spontaneous and step outside of our comfort zone.

GODDESS RITUAL

As water is so important to this goddess, you can connect to her power by using it in a ritual to enhance creativity. Gather together objects that are sacred to Yemoja, for example shells, a piece of quartz, and a blue bead. Flowers are also linked to this goddess, particularly white or blue blooms, so you might prefer to take a flower with you. Write any wishes or requests that you have on a piece of paper. Next, find a body of flowing water, such as a river or a stream. Take the objects you have gathered, including your written request, and cast them into the water. Imagine the goddess rising up from the depths and blowing you a kiss.

GODDESS WISDOM
To increase personal power and strength, take a piece of the skin of a watermelon (after eating) and carve your initials into the flesh. Leave it to dry and then carry it with you as a protective charm.

Sun & Moon

Deities of the Sun and Moon are among the most dynamic. These magnificent beings will teach you how to make the most of any situation, and how to achieve your wildest dreams. Like the planets that rule them, they offer light and illumination in any situation. They bring blessings of warmth, joy, and a wealth of good fortune, as well as insight into the areas in your life that need attention.

Mystical and magical in every sense of the word, these goddesses help us to harness the power of the universe, and develop our inner strength and intuition. They show us that we have, at our fingertips, everything we need truly to excel and reach our goals.

Tap into their power by standing beneath the light of the Sun and Moon. Embrace the energy of these planets and imagine it covering you from head to toe. Anything is possible when working with these deities. All it takes to move mountains is a little imagination, some self-belief, and a sprinkling of faith.

Áine

PLANET
Sun, Moon

STONE
Citrine, quartz, moonstone

FOOD / DRINK
Bread, flour, blackberries

FLOWER / PLANT
Mistletoe, oak tree, hawthorn

SCENT
Blackberry, blackcurrant

ANIMAL TOTEM
Red mare, rabbit, swan

MISCELLANEOUS
White flowers, the flame or torch, fire, magic ring

The people of Ireland revered this gorgeous Celtic goddess. Her name means "bright," which is why she is often referred to as the "spark" or "flame of life". She had a light, frivolous energy, associated with love, creativity, fertility, and abundance. Áine was closely linked to Cnoc Áine, a hill in County Limerick. This auspicious place was sacred to the Irish, and the people would gather here in honor of the goddess. In particular, Áine was responsible for nourishing the soil, helping the crops to grow, and the cattle to flourish, and the celebrations reflected this. Many rituals involved lighting fires and running through the fields with torches to bless them for the year ahead.

Áine was called the Faerie Queen of Munster, and had close links with the world of faerie. Midsummer was the best time to worship her and ask for her blessing. Once the festivities had died down, it was thought that Áine would appear with her faerie cohort, and they would dance around the summit of the hill. One story tells of how a group of young girls were playing by Áine's hill late one night, when the goddess appeared to them. She flashed them a beautiful smile, and then opened her cloak to reveal a portal to the otherworld. She warned the girls that they should go home before her faerie friends arrived as, if they did not, they would be drawn into faerie land, never to be seen again. Many believed that Áine possessed a magical ring that enabled the wearer to see faeries.

In some tales, she was a mortal woman who had been enchanted by faeries, and over the years she and a number of faerie men produced a half-human, half-faerie race. Often appearing as a red mare that no one could outrun, Áine is also associated with a red bull, which would appear by her side on the hill. Traditionally a Sun goddess, Áine is also linked to the Moon, and has many powers, including shapeshifting and enchanting mortals.

She is so adaptable, you can work with Áine in any area of your life. She will help create abundance, and get things moving. Her message is one of energy and creativity. She teaches us that we have all we need to create the life we want. The spark of light, the ideas, and the intent are within us. We only have to learn how to use them.

GODDESS RITUAL

One of the best ways to encourage the flow of prosperity and success into your life is to perform this simple bread-baking ritual to Áine. You can use a bread maker, or if you prefer, have a go at baking bread yourself. As the dough rises, imagine your bank balance increasing. See yourself becoming more and more successful. While the bread is cooking, picture yourself achieving your dream and imagine how it would feel to be successful and prosperous. Say: "Áine, shower me with success, my energy grows, I am truly blessed." Now eat the bread, and enjoy those feelings of fulfillment.

GODDESS WISDOM

Keep a vase of white flowers on your windowsill, beneath the light of the sun and moon. To enhance Áine's energy in your life, you might also want to add a piece of citrine and an image of a horse, rabbit, or swan.

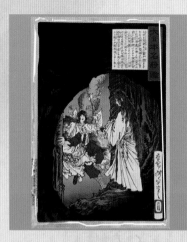

Amaterasu

This beautiful Japanese Sun goddess is linked to growth and compassion. Associated with the fields of rice that fed the population, it was her job to illuminate the world, and help the crops grow. An accomplished weaver, she is also linked to the ornate satins and silks which were used to make gowns for the people.   A sensitive soul, Amaterasu was deeply hurt when her brother Susanowa, the storm god, went on a rampage, killing a horse (an animal sacred to the goddess) and dumping its body in her weaving room.

Amaterasu, shocked and depressed by her brother's actions, fled to a cave in the mountains where she hid her light from the world. As a result of this, the rice fields began to die, and the people were hungry. The other deities tried to encourage her to return to the world, but she was too distraught. In the end it was the fun-loving goddess Uzumu who succeeded, just by making her laugh. She flipped over a barrel at the mouth of the cave and began to dance upon it, making a thundering sound with her feet, and acting the clown. Amaterasu was so intrigued by the noise that she crept to the entrance for a closer look. While she was distracted, the other gods sealed the mouth of the cave so she couldn't hide her light any more.

Amaterasu shows great compassion in all she does, and her message is one of love.

PLANET
The Sun and also Venus

STONE
Quartz or glass
(anything that reflects the sun's rays)

FOOD / DRINK
Rice

FLOWER / PLANT
Orchid

SCENT
Sandalwood

ANIMAL TOTEM
Horse

MISCELLANEOUS
Mirror, loom, arrow, silk or satin,
thread, images of the rising sun

GODDESS RITUAL

To radiate love and beauty and give yourself a "feel good" boost, tap into the energizing power of Amaterasu. Take a compact mirror and leave it on your window ledge for five minutes to catch the first rays of the morning sun. Wrap it in a satin or silk scarf and place it beneath a vase of colorful flowers. Every day spend five minutes gazing into this mirror. Imagine the rays of the sun bathing your face in golden light. Smile and say: "I shine like the Sun goddess Amaterasu, my light grows brighter with all that I do!"

AMATERASU

Sunna

This enchanting Norse Sun goddess brings light and warmth to every occasion. She is often thought to be a representation of Sol, although in some tales Sol appears to be Sunna's mother. When the world was created, Sunna was born from a spark sent forth from the Land of Fire. Each day, she rides through the sky in a chariot pulled by a pair of horses, the Allsvinn. These horses are very fast, which is just as well since the chariot is closely pursued by the terrifying wolf Skoll. Sometimes Skoll gets so close to Sunna he is able to get his jaws around the Sun and take a bite, causing a solar eclipse.

Sister of Mani, the Moon god, and wife of Glen, whose name means "shine," Sunna is a caring deity, who has the ability to heal. In Norse mythology, the story goes that at the end of the world, a time known as Ragnarok, the Sun will eventually be caught and swallowed whole by Skoll. When this happens, a new and improved world will emerge, where peace reigns and the Sun shines even brighter with the help of this glorious goddess.

Also called All Bright, Ever Glow, and Fair Wheel, this beautiful deity represents light and energy. In one tale, she begins life as a human child. Her father is so captivated by her that he decides to name her after the brightest star. This angers the gods in Asgard. As punishment, they take her up to the heavens where she remains, riding her chariot through the sky every day.

PLANET
Sun

STONE
Citrine, amber

FOOD / DRINK
Sunflower seeds, orange, lemon

FLOWER / PLANT
Sunflower, yellow flowers of any kind

SCENT
Orange, lemon, citronella

ANIMAL TOTEM
Horse

MISCELLANEOUS
The colors gold and orange, wheel, transport of any kind

Her two faithful equine companions are protected from the heat of the Sun by a talisman created by Odin. This talisman hangs from their yoke and produces a cooling mist, which prevents them from being burned. Since Sunna is most often pictured driving her chariot through the sky, she is closely associated with travel and movement, and governs these areas.

Sunna's message is one of warmth. She teaches us that real beauty comes from within. We all have a light to shine. The key is learning to love and accept yourself.

GODDESS RITUAL

To attract happiness and good fortune into your world, perform this ritual in honor of Sunna. Take an orange candle and a tablespoon of sunflower oil. Massage the oil into the wax of the candle while thinking about the generous light of the Sun. Take a pin and carve the word "joy" into the flesh of the candle. Finally, light the candle. As the flame grows, picture a spark of light within your chest area. Feel it stretching and filling you with warmth. Imagine your aura, the energy field that surrounds your body, getting brighter like the light of the Sun.

GODDESS WISDOM

To invite Sunna's warmth and vitality into your life, incorporate some citrus fruits in your diet. Drink orange juice first thing in the morning, or if you prefer, hot water and a generous squeeze of lemon, and ask the goddess to bless you with energy and vigour for the rest of the day.

Isis

The Mother of Life, Isis was a dazzling deity with myriad powers. Known as the goddess of magic, she had infinite wisdom, which she used to her advantage to gain the powers of the Sun god, Ra. Unlike other Egyptian deities, Isis was keen to mix with her people, teaching them how to grow corn, weave, and use medicine. Wife of Osiris and mother of the Sun god, Horus, she embodied the nurturing qualities of love, and was often associated with rebirth because she could bring the dead back to life.

A Moon goddess and a great sorceress, Isis incorporated elements of the trickster in her dealings with others. She created a snake out of mud and saliva to bite Ra, and then offered to heal him, but to overcome such powerful magic she needed his secret magical name. True to her word, she saved Ra, and in learning his secret name she became the most powerful goddess in Egypt. She used this to her advantage, caring for and protecting the people.

Isis let her intuition guide her at all times, and could easily read people, which made her an excellent communicator. Often pictured wearing a throne upon her head to indicate her regal status, her image adorns many ancient Egyptian artefacts. As a guide to the underworld she was pictured with outstretched wings. This popular symbol of protection was used on the royal throne to symbolize her support for each ruler.

Isis shows us the importance of knowledge, of learning and of broadening our horizons. Her power is in her ability to connect with

PLANET
Moon

STONE
Lapis lazuli

FOOD / DRINK
Corn, wheat, bread

FLOWER / PLANT
Cedar, lotus

SCENT
Cinnamon

ANIMAL TOTEM
Sparrowhawk, sometimes snake

MISCELLANEOUS
Ankh, full Moon, throne, rivers
(particularly the Nile)

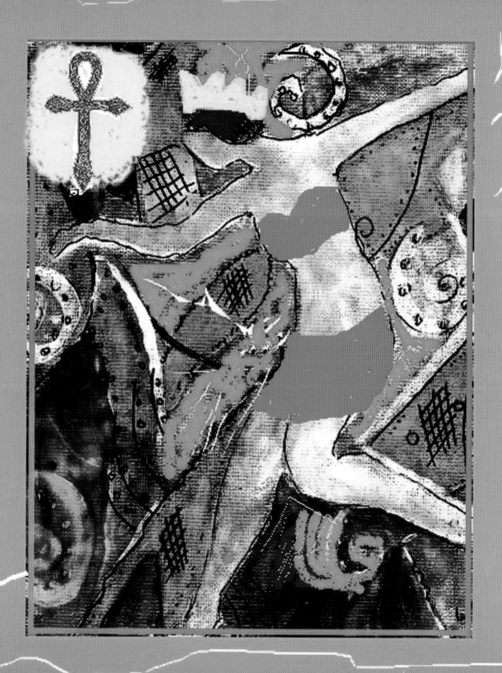

people, and in having a keen sixth sense. She teaches us to trust our instincts. Work with Isis to hone intuition and develop psychic powers.

GODDESS RITUAL

Increase your magical powers and flex those intuitive muscles with this Isis ritual. Add a couple of drops of cinnamon oil to a small bowl of hot water and inhale the fragrance. Close your eyes and visualize a golden lotus flower on top of your head. This is the gateway to your subconscious mind. Picture the petals of the flower opening. In the center is a spinning blue orb. Feel the healing blue light pass down into your forehead and through the rest of your body. Relax and let any thoughts or images come to you. When you've finished, imagine the flower closing again. Keep a journal and make a note of anything you remember. It may prove to be a useful insight into the future.

GODDESS WISDOM

Spend time beneath the light of the full Moon, and learn about its different phases. Stand tall with your arms outstretched, and ask Isis to bless and protect you.

$\mathcal{B}ast$

PLANET
Sun and Moon

STONE
Moonstone, tiger's eye

FOOD / DRINK
Cinnamon, milk

FLOWER / PLANT
Catnip, yew, cypress

SCENT
Cinnamon, frankincense, musk

ANIMAL TOTEM
Cats of all sizes

MISCELLANEOUS
Rising sun, the all-seeing eye, perfume
jars, music and dancing

Powerful and super sleek, Bast is the Egyptian goddess of cats, and a protector of women. Often pictured with a cat's head on a female form, Bast, sometimes known as Bastet, is the embodiment of grace and strength. This versatile deity governs health, the home, and sensual pleasure. A real party diva, she is associated with all forms of music, dance, and celebration.

Also known as the All-Seeing Eye, or the Lady of the East, Bast had another role, which was to protect her father, the Sun god Ra. By day she would ride in his chariot through the sky, by night she'd rise up against the evil serpent demon Apep, her father's nemesis. Her all-seeing eye shone through the darkness, making her an excellent predator, and she was also able to light up the world and keep the soil warm and fertile. Her solar power and her ability to see at night mean that she is considered both a Sun and a Moon goddess.

Cats were sacred to the ancient Egyptians and Bast's status as a cat goddess meant that they were under her protection at all times. Many households would have a small bronze statue of the goddess, or her All-Seeing Eye, as a way of protecting the home from intruders. The Egyptians believed her talents had no end and she was also worshipped as a fertility goddess, whose powers included easing the pain of childbirth.

Having had three husbands and countless lovers, Bast was considered generous with her sexual favors and seen as a pleasure-

seeking deity. Part of her innate attraction was her independence and an ability to enjoy herself freely, in any situation.

Bast's lesson is one of independence and versatility. She teaches us to love life, face our fears, and embrace the spirit of freedom.

GODDESS RITUAL

Increase your powers of perception with this enchanting ritual. Start by burning some cinnamon oil or adding a couple of drops to a bowl of hot water. Inhale the aroma and relax. Close your eyes and imagine you have a third, cat's eye in the center of your forehead. Picture it opening and shining gold. As you breathe in, imagine that this eye is taking in positive energy, and as you breathe out, imagine that it's releasing any negative emotions. Say: "My senses are alive, my spirit shines so bright. My heart is filled with love, my life is filled with light!"

GODDESS WISDOM

To tap into Bast's power, and boost confidence, play your favorite song, and dance to it. Close your eyes and get lost in the rhythm while picturing yourself bathed in the sun's rays.

Hecate

This enigmatic and extremely powerful Greek goddess is a Moon deity and also a triple goddess, meaning she embraces aspects of the Mother, the Maiden, and the Crone and can appear in all three forms. Hecate (Trivia) is the ultimate multitasker, taking on a number of roles, including queen of the witches and goddess of the crossroads. As a testament to her power, she's the only one of the old deities that Zeus allowed to reign in his newly formed Mount Olympus. He gave her the power to grant wishes to humankind. Ruling Earth, sky, and sea, Hecate also had an influence on the weather, making her a favorite goddess of shepherds and sailors.

Unlike many other deities, she never married, preferring a life of solitude and wisdom. Hecate was known to wander the streets at night, a luminous figure with skin like the Moon. Her favorite places were cemeteries and crossroads, where she'd spend time conjuring magic. In her guise as queen of the witches, Hecate ruled magic in all its forms. She was gifted in divination and could see into the past and the future. For this reason, she is often thought of as the goddess of mystics and seers.

A great friend and confidante to the goddess Persephone, she traveled the realms of the underworld, and was able to converse with the spirits that lived there. Associated with the dark phase of the Moon, Hecate was often pictured with an owl as her companion.

PLANET
Moon

STONE
Smoky quartz, obsidian, moonstone

FOOD / DRINK
Currants, raisins, honey

FLOWER / PLANT
Willows, glades of trees

SCENT
Lemon, cypress

ANIMAL TOTEM
Owl, dog, bat, horse

MISCELLANEOUS
Crossroads, candles, the number 3

Those who wished to petition her help would do so by leaving food or other offerings at a crossroads after midnight. Sometimes they would erect a pole in this spot, and tie up three masks, to represent the triple nature of the goddess.

Working with Hecate will enhance natural intuition and help you tap into your higher self. Her lesson is one of quiet understanding and knowledge. She teaches us to let go of the things we no longer need and shows us that a balance of light and dark will enable us to find true peace and enlightenment.

GODDESS RITUAL

To overcome obstacles or break a bad habit, try this simple ritual to the goddess. Gather together a handful of currants and raisins and a couple of lemon pips. Take them to a crossroads at night and sprinkle them in a circle on the ground. If there isn't a crossroads where you live, perform the ritual in your garden or local park. Spin around three times and say: "Hecate, by the power of three, take this burden away from me. Give me strength to move with grace, release the past, and make good haste!" Visualize your problem melting away and thank the goddess for her help.

GODDESS WISDOM
An easy way to attract Hecate's attention is to light a white candle and leave it burning on your windowsill beneath the light of the moon. Make a wish for Hecate's blessing, and let the candle burn down naturally.

Artemis

This wild Greek goddess of the hunt was also a Moon goddess, and often referred to as goddess of light. The ultimate nature lover, she would run with the beasts of the wood and was happiest when spending time outdoors. Daughter of the god Zeus, and a powerful deity of protection, Artemis (Diana) looked after women and wild animals in equal measure. A bold spirit with a strong sense of freedom, Artemis wasn't afraid to stand up for herself. When the hunter Actaeon found her bathing in a stream, she turned him into a stag for peeking at her naked body. She also turned one of her nymphs, Callisto, into a bear on discovering that she'd had an affair with Zeus. Luckily for the poor nymph, Zeus intervened and transformed her into the constellation of stars we now know as "the bear."

Since she is associated with the moon, Artemis is often pictured carrying a torch or candle. It is her responsibility to light the path for others, to provide illumination and protection at all times. Her bow and arrow were always at her side, and she was a skilled huntress. Often pictured in the company of her nymphs, bathing or running through the woods, Artemis wasn't as interested in matters of the heart as some of her counterparts. However, she did have one true love—Orion. Her brother, Apollo, was jealous of his sister's close relationship with the mortal man. So he tricked her into killing him by setting her a challenge to shoot a tiny speck moving in the river

PLANET
Moon

STONE
Moonstone

FOOD / DRINK
Berries and nuts

FLOWER / PLANT
Trees of any kind, honeysuckle

SCENT
Lavender, mint, honey

ANIMAL TOTEM
Dog, stag, horse, bee

MISCELLANEOUS
Crescent moon, bow and arrow,
woods and forests, candles

many miles away. The speck happened to be Orion, swimming, but Artemis didn't know this, and being adept with the bow and arrow, she shot and killed him. When she realized what she'd done, she turned him into a constellation of stars and fired him into the sky where he remains to this day. Other tales tell quite a different story of her relationship with Orion. One suggests that he tried to rape her and so she killed him with her bow and arrow and turned him into the constellation.

Worshipped as a fertility goddess, Artemis had a softer, caring side, and a deep passion for helping the vulnerable and needy. Her message today is one of freedom. She teaches us to be true to ourselves, to follow our dreams and our heart, and to look after our animal friends.

GODDESS RITUAL

To inspire confidence and help you pursue your dreams, carry out this ritual to Artemis. Gather a handful of fresh lavender, some berries and nuts, and go out walking. Find a spot near a tree, in a wood or park, or if you prefer, you can do this in your own garden. Sprinkle the lavender, nuts, and berries in a circle at the base of the tree. Sit beneath its branches, close your eyes, and ask Artemis to free your soul. Imagine the bark of the tree supporting you. Feel the warm energy travel up your spine, giving you the confidence to follow your dreams.

GODDESS WISDOM

Take up an active pastime that takes you outside and helps you connect with animals, such as horse riding, bird watching, or even walking the dog. Wear animal prints and jewelry. Give thanks for your animal friends and ask Artemis to protect you all.

Selene

PLANET
Moon

STONE
Moonstone

FOOD / DRINK
Milk

FLOWER / PLANT
Willow tree

SCENT
Myrtle, rose

ANIMAL TOTEM
Horse, ox

MISCELLANEOUS
Poetry, full Moon, the color white

This radiant Greek goddess of the Moon was often pictured in white, wearing the Moon upon her head in its crescent form. At night, she would rise from the sea in a chariot pulled by two white-winged horses. They would gallop across the sky, spreading her luminescence for the entire world to see. Some tales describe Selene as being pulled by oxen, and her crescent-Moon crown resembling a pair of white horns. A triple goddess, Selene represents the Mother aspect, although she could equally well appear as Maiden or Crone, depending on the situation. She is a symbol of fertility and feminine strength and was worshipped for these qualities, usually around the time of the full Moon.

Selene had many admirers and love affairs. One of her most prominent liaisons was with the god Zeus. She also fell madly in love with a mortal man, Endymion, whom she saw one night as she rode her chariot across the sky. Selene knew that, unlike her, Endymion would age and eventually die, so she petitioned Zeus for his help, and asked him to grant her lover eternal sleep, knowing that if she asked for eternal life, he was bound to trick her or do the opposite and end Endymion's life. Zeus took pity on Selene and decided to grant her wish. From that day forward, Endymion spent his days and nights in deep slumber, dreaming about the Moon. Meanwhile, Selene bore him fifty daughters, who symbolize the fifty lunar months between each Olympic Games. Selene is often linked to love because of this romantic tale, and is also seen as a goddess of inspiration, particularly to poets and those with amorous tendencies.

Selene's message is one of hope. She embraces love and teaches us to hold on to those who are dear to us. Like the Moon that inspires so many, she urges us to express ourselves, to show how we really feel, and to cherish our loved ones.

GODDESS RITUAL

To give and receive love unconditionally, tap into Selene's power with this easy ritual. When the Moon is waxing (getting larger), pour a glass of milk and add a couple of ice cubes. Leave it on a window ledge beneath the light of the Moon for a few minutes. Imagine the milk absorbing the light from the Moon's rays. When you're ready, stand beneath the Moon and picture a shower of white light pouring over you. Sip the milk slowly and say: "Selene, your light has filled me up, I am an overflowing cup of love and joy and romance sweet. Upon this night I am complete."

GODDESS WISDOM

Unleash your poetic side and get creative with the help of Selene. By the light of the full Moon, sit with pen and paper, and let any thoughts pour out. Start by describing the Moon, and then give your ideas a rhythmic slant and begin to join them up until you have a poem. Start a poetic journal, and use it to jot down your thoughts.

"Selene, your light has filled me up,
I am an overflowing cup of love
and joy and romance sweet.
Upon this night I am complete."

Rhiannon

This captivating Welsh goddess of the Moon was also a queen of
the faeries. She would appear on faerie mounds, or Tors as they
were often called, wearing a gown of gold, and sometimes on
horseback. Although she was promised to another deity, Rhiannon
was in love with a mortal man, Prince Pwyll. In an attempt to seduce
him, she appeared many times on a particular Tor, when he was out
hunting. Pwyll was dazzled by her beauty and chased after her every
time, but her horse was too fast and she disappeared into the
otherworld before he could get close. Eventually, after he cried out
to her, she stopped and they spoke and agreed to be married.

Although the marriage should have been a happy one, the birth
of their child brought much sorrow for Rhiannon. Unlike the other
women of the court, she was always an outsider. When her baby
disappeared one night while she slept, the other women hatched a
cunning plan. They smeared her clothes in blood and left bones
nearby to make it look as if she'd murdered her own child. Pwyll
was horrified by his wife's actions, but he couldn't bring himself to
sentence her to death. Instead, she was chained to the castle gates,
wearing a horse's collar around her neck. It was her punishment
to carry visitors to the castle upon her back. Although Rhiannon was
innocent of any crime, she bore her punishment with humility and
her reputation as a goddess of virtue and strength grew.   Eventually,
she was vindicated, and her child, who had been kidnapped, was
returned.

PLANET
Moon, Sun

STONE
Moonstone, quartz

FOOD / DRINK
Sage

FLOWER / PLANT
Jasmine, any white flower

SCENT
Jasmine, geranium

ANIMAL TOTEM
White horse, songbirds

MISCELLANEOUS
The colors gold and silver, gate,
horseshoe, the number 7

Rhiannon is often thought of as the ultimate mother goddess by the Celts. Followers call upon her powers of healing and forgiveness. Associated with the dream world and magic, she is often accompanied by golden songbirds that can raise the dead and comfort the living.

Rhiannon's message is one of forgiveness. She champions unconditional love and healing, and the ability to see both sides of the story. She can also help you develop the power of prophecy.

GODDESS RITUAL

To cleanse body and soul and release past hurts, try this ritual to Rhiannon. Take a handful of fresh sage and steep it in hot water. Add a couple of drops of geranium essential oil. Inhale the aroma, and waft the steam around your body. Imagine it cleansing your aura from top to toe. Finally, picture a golden cloak about your shoulders, protecting you and increasing your personal power. Say: "Past hurts are gone, I now move on. My heart is healed, my true path revealed."

Repeat this chant seven times in honor of Rhiannon.

GODDESS WISDOM

Develop stamina and determination by tapping into Rhiannon's power. Horses are important to her, and a symbol of true strength and tenacity. Place a horseshoe near the entrance to your home, and invest in images of horses galloping forward. Make a simple charm by drawing a horseshoe in gold ink and keeping it with you.

"Past hurts are gone, I now move on. My heart is healed, my true path revealed."

Fire & Ice

The wondrous deities of fire and ice will inspire you to move forward, step outside your comfort zone, and be proud of who you are. Resolute and bold, these awesome creatures aren't afraid of anything. They encourage us to take that first brave step into a new life, and make the best of what we've got. Talented and charming, they know how to get what they want, because they know how to make others feel special. Working their magic with a smile or a positive word, they will lift your spirits and help you soar above the clouds. Tap into their power by being spontaneous. Make room for surprises in your life, and make a point of doing something different every day. These vibrant beings teach us to celebrate our unique gifts. They help us follow our passion and aim for the stars. Most importantly, they teach us to reach out to others so that they may see how truly fabulous they are, too.

Juno

PLANET
Jupiter

STONE
Diamond, garnet

FOOD / DRINK
Coconut, wine

FLOWER / PLANT
Poppy, cypress

SCENT
Myrrh, frankincense

ANIMAL TOTEM
Peacock, cow

MISCELLANEOUS
Coins, money, marriage, tiara

This Roman goddess, often referred to as queen of the gods, was the daughter of Saturn and married to her brother, Jupiter. Despite her strange family tree, the Roman people named the month of June after her and held her in high regard. Like her husband, she had the power to throw lightning bolts, which would prove useful in her guise as goddess of war. Often pictured wearing a goatskin coat, and ready for battle, she was popular with Roman warriors who petitioned her for help and courage. Juno (Hera) was also a goddess of conception, and was called upon during pregnancy and labor. A protector of women and linked to marriage, she could be summoned to settle marital disputes and disagreements. She was commonly known as goddess of the mint, looking after the finances of the Roman people. Rome was her city, and she had a temple on the Arx, or citadel, close to the Royal Mint.

Like the mother matriarch, Juno was efficient, reliable, and wise, and with her organized, no-nonsense attitude, it's easy to see why she was well loved. She is often pictured wearing a diadem on her head to represent her regal status, and is closely associated with the peacock. Her presence could be found in many towns in ancient Italy, where temples and shrines were built in her honor.

As she is a goddess of marriage, many people consider June to be the perfect month in which to marry in order to ensure a long and happy relationship. Juno's message is one of organization. She is a strong and methodical adversary, operating with military precision

and great firepower. She teaches us to be ready for action, to investigate every avenue, and to experience life to the fullest. She promotes love and honesty, and will help you progress in every area of life.

GODDESS RITUAL

To help you achieve your full potential and make your dreams come true, try this ritual to Juno. Take a pinch of myrrh and a handful of frankincense and place them in a fireproof bowl. On a piece of paper, write one or two words to sum up your dream, this could be "true love," "new job," or "money." Place the paper in the bowl. Light a match and say: "With Juno's blessing my dreams are coming true, from this day, in everything I do." Drop the match in the bowl, and imagine it's a bolt of lightning sent to transport your dreams to the heavens. Let the contents burn while thinking about how you will achieve your goal.

GODDESS WISDOM

Juno knows how to prepare herself for battle. If you're facing a challenge, or need a confidence boost, invest in some coconut oil. Massage into your skin while imagining that you're covered in golden armor. Rinse off in the shower and continue to visualize yourself protected from head to foot.

"With Juno's blessing my dreams are coming true, from this day, in everything I do."

Hestia

The Greek goddess of hearth and home, Hestia (Vesta) is linked to the kinder aspects of fire. This nurturing deity governs domesticity. Her name means "the essence," and she represents the value of the family, the most important aspects of family life, and the security and comfort of home. She was one of the most powerful deities of the Greek Pantheon. Her strength lay in her calm nature, which at first appeared mild but soon developed into quiet determination. She was the goddess of hospitality, known for extending the hand of friendship and offering comfort. The sacred flame is associated with Hestia, and the circle is her symbol, because it represents the notion that she is complete within herself.

Daughter of Cronus and Rhea, she was the first-born and also the last After her father heard a propehcy that one of his children would take his throne, he quickly swallowed her at birth. When his child Zeus was born, Cronus was tricked into swallowing a rock covered in swaddling clothes instead of his son The young god Zeus was hidden away from his father until he was grown. He then returned and forced Cronus to disgorge everything he had swallowed. Hestia, being the first-born and thus the first swallowed, was the last to come out. She is often called the first and last.

Despite her traumatic beginnings, Hestia grew to be a beautiful and confident goddess, attracting the attention of both Apollo and Poseidon. But Hestia knew her own heart, and declared that she would not marry. Instead, she would remain at home, keeping it in

PLANET
Earth

STONE
Garnet, gold

FOOD / DRINK
Bread

FLOWER / PLANT
Chamomile, basil

SCENT
Lavender

ANIMAL TOTEM
Pig, donkey, horse

MISCELLANEOUS
Hearth, flame, fireplace, altar, oven, keys

order, and making sure that there was always a fire in the hearth and a warm welcome for everyone. Hestia is thought to have governed the household, ensuring supplies were always carefully managed. She is also the goddess of architecture. In ancient Greece it was thought that all homes were built from the center outward because this was where the hearth and Hestia's sacred flame were found.

Hestia's message is one of generosity and warmth, of reaching out to strangers, and of living in peace and harmony with one other. She teaches us to be humble and kind in every situation.

GODDESS RITUAL

Encourage a happy home, and eliminate any bad vibes with this Hestia ritual. Steep a handful of fresh basil and chamomile leaves in a cup of boiling water for five minutes. Strain and add to your usual floor wash. Take a mop and clean your floors in a circular motion, while repeating the following chant: "Hestia blesses my home with warmth, she lights up every corner with joy!" Pay special attention to your front and back step and the main entrance to your home. As you mop, picture a stream of golden light flowing through your house, bringing joy and prosperity.

GODDESS WISDOM

De-stress and relax by adding three or four drops of lavender essential oil to a hot flannel and placing it over your forehead. Breathe deeply, and ask Hestia to bring you warmth, peace, and security.

"Hestia blesses my home with warmth, she lights up every corner with joy!"

Pele

PLANET
Mars

STONE
Carnelian

FOOD / DRINK
Peppers

FLOWER / PLANT
Flowers from the Ohi'a Lehua tree

SCENT
Patchouli

ANIMAL TOTEM
Dog (usually white)

MISCELLANEOUS
Fire, lava, volcano, mountain

This Hawaiian fire goddess wears her heart on her sleeve and delivers her own brand of justice. Originally destined to be a water goddess, Pele soon changed her mind, becoming obsessed with the tempestuous nature of fire. One of her favorite pastimes as a child was to play with the flames of the underworld, and, during one such game, she even set her home—the island of Tahiti—alight. Linked to volcanoes, lava, and anything hot, Pele tested followers by pretending to be an old woman in need of assistance. She would appear on the mountainside, looking lost and confused. Those who helped her and offered kindness received blessings of love, but those who refused were surrounded by seething lava.

Swift to get angry, but just as quick to forgive, Pele is known for her jealous streak. Tales tell of her fascination with a handsome mortal man, Ohi'a. He refused to fall for Pele's seductive advances because he was in love with a mortal woman, Lehua. Pele flew into a terrible rage at this rejection and killed both lovers as punishment. But her erratic nature meant she soon regretted her actions, and reunited the lovers for eternity by turning Ohi'a into a tree and filling the branches with the lovely Lehua flower. The Ohi'a Lehua tree is sacred to Pele, and is able to sprout beautiful flowers despite the hard earth of the lava bed.

Pele has the ability to shapeshift into the form of a white dog, an old woman, or a young maiden with long dark hair and red eyes. There have been many sightings of this goddess over the years.

A creative force of nature, Pele teaches us to embrace our passion, go with the flow, and express ourselves creatively. We may not always get what we want, but Pele shows us that we can turn things around, and that there is the potential for growth and movement in any situation. All it takes is a change of attitude, and the spark of an idea.

GODDESS RITUAL

White is Pele's color. She is often pictured wearing flowing white robes. As a deity she governs matters of the heart, so if you have a love request, write it down and light a white candle. Burn the paper in the flame while saying: "Pele's power flows through me, ignites the flame of destiny. As I say, so it shall be. My wish fulfilled and sent to me." Keep the ashes in a box with a piece of carnelian to attract love and passion into your life. When your wish has come true, sprinkle the ashes outside and repeat the chant.

Astrape

The illuminating Greek goddess of lightning, Astrape, is often pictured standing behind or at the side of the great god Zeus as he sits on his throne. This shows her standing, strength, and power among the other deities. A stunning goddess not to be taken lightly, Astrape had brightly shining eyes that could flash a lightning bolt within seconds of looking at you. She wields a flaming torch and is often seen with an aureole upon her head.

In the great battle between gods and titans, Astrape supported the gods, and fought at the side of Zeus. Some tales say that she was his attendant, carrying his thunderbolts in her arms. He granted her a place in the heavens because of her loyalty, and she appears as the constellation Virgo. Images show her wearing a gown adorned with sparkling stars, and she is often referred to as Astraea, which means "starry."

An honorable and virtuous deity, Astrape is associated with justice, and was called upon to soothe conflicts and help those unfairly treated She is often swathed in gold, with a beautiful light around her head, and two huge wings. Today she can be called upon when justice is needed. She will shed light upon a situation and help you to see the truth. Her lesson is one of obedience, of doing what is right, and of offering help and support to others. She teaches us to look out for one other, to be honest in all our dealings, and to hold friendship dearly.

PLANET
Mars

STONE
Gold, iron pyrite

FOOD / DRINK
Water

FLOWER / PLANT
Any yellow flower

SCENT
Lemon, lemon verbena

ANIMAL TOTEM
Any bird

MISCELLANEOUS
Stars, torch, flame, thunder and lightning

GODDESS RITUAL

If you're confused and need some illumination in any area of your life, try this ritual to Astrape. Take a lemon and cut it in half. Say: "The truth is revealed with light and love." Squeeze the juice into a bowl and add some hot water and a couple of drops of lemon-verbena essential oil. Place a towel over your head, and inhale the fresh aroma. Close your eyes and picture a giant star in front of you. See it sparkling with gold light. Imagine stepping into the star and becoming a part of it. Feel yourself shimmering with joy, strength, and clarity. Say: "Astrape, goddess of the stars, help me see what must be. Help me shine my inner light to free me from my current plight!"

GODDESS WISDOM

If you want to forge friendships that last, take a tip from Astrape. Use the power of your eyes to engage and mesmerize. As you hold your friend's gaze, imagine a bolt made of light and love passing between you. In your mind, say the word that captures your message — it might be "love," "happiness," or "friendship"—and then smile.

Brigid

The Celtic goddess of fire rules the hearth and forge and governs inspiration and poetry. A talented and beautiful deity, she has been associated with the Christian Saint Brigid since the Middle Ages. According to legend, she was born at daybreak and rose into the sky, rays of fiery flames about her head. Daughter of the great god Dagda, who was the father of Ireland, this magical child was fed with the milk of the Sacred Cow in the otherworld. Brigid spent much of her childhood in the otherworld, where she had her own apple orchard and magical bees that transported their nectar to the real world. A true flower maiden, wherever she walked fresh flowers would spring instantly from the ground. This was a sign of her power and fertility.

Brigid is often linked to springs and wells. The Celts believed that water was a portal into the otherworld, and could also provide inspiration and healing. One tale tells of two lepers who came to visit the goddess at her well in Kildare. They were desperate to be healed and Brigid took pity on them, advising them to bathe each other from head to toe in the magical water. The first leper, once healed, was repulsed by his friend and refused to bathe him. Brigid was so annoyed by his behavior that she caused his leprosy to return She then placed her cloak around the shoulders of the second leper and healed him.

As a wise woman and teacher, Brigid showed humans how to gather herbs to heal the sick and how to forge tools of iron She was

PLANET
Sun

STONE
Agate, jasper

FOOD / DRINK
Pumpkin seeds, oats, nuts, sage

FLOWER / PLANT
Snowdrop, oak tree

SCENT
Lavender, lemon verbena, apple

ANIMAL TOTEM
Bee, cow, lamb

MISCELLANEOUS
Fire, candles, spring, well, bell

the poet's muse, and the patroness of midwifery, protecting women in childbirth and looking out for their children. A complex yet loving goddess, her message is one of unity and healing, of developing a creative nature, and of spreading love and happiness to the world.

GODDESS RITUAL

To improve health and vitality, enlist Brigid's help with this simple ritual. Take a handful of freshly chopped sage and simmer in a pan of boiling water for ten minutes. Strain the liquid into a mug. Add a spoonful of honey and a squeeze of fresh lemon juice. Sip slowly while picturing your body surrounded by a cloak of fire. Feel the warmth penetrate your skin, giving you a burst of energy and healing any aches or pains. Say: "Brigid, fiery goddess that you are, thank you for your blessing, for this healing from afar." Perform this ritual every morning to set you up for the day.

GODDESS WISDOM

For inspiration and an insight into the future, fill a dark colored bowl with water. Add a drop of lavender essential oil, and spend a few moments gazing into the depths. Let your eyes relax and let any images or patterns develop. Make a note of anything that appears.

Skadi

This impressive Viking goddess of winter proved to be a formidable force with men and gods alike. Her name is said to mean "shadow" and she is sometimes referred to as Queen of the Shades. A giantess who governs snow, ice, and all things wintry, she is associated with mountains and skiing, and is often depicted wearing huge snowshoes or skates, which she used to navigate the snowy landscape while hunting.

A no-nonsense deity, Skadi is most famous for standing up to the Norse gods of Asgard. After they murdered her father, she stormed their court and demanded justice. The gods, who must have been intimidated by her presence, decided to let her choose one of them as her future husband. The only problem was that none of them really wanted to marry her. To make things interesting, they said she must pick her spouse by looking only at his feet. Skadi agreed to the challenge because she was secretly in love with the handsome god Balder. Thinking he would have the nicest looking feet, she chose the most beautiful, which turned out to belong to Njord, the god of the sea. The marriage was doomed to failure, not only because of the lack of affection, but also because Njord loved his realm of the sea and Skadi, her snow-capped mountains. They could not agree where to live, and neither was happy in the other's realm. In the end, they agreed to part, but all was not lost for Skadi. She went on to have several sons with the god Odin.

Other tales paint Skadi in a different light, calling her a hideous troll woman, who would castrate and collect the penises of heroes.

PLANET
Saturn

STONE
Obsidian, any kind of metal

FOOD / DRINK
Ice cream, water, milk, pear

FLOWER / PLANT
Snowdrop

SCENT
Myrrh, juniper

ANIMAL TOTEM
Wolf, snake, arctic fox

MISCELLANEOUS
Snow, mountains, skis, scythe

Skadi's passion and spirit give us strength in the darkest of times, those wintry moments of our life. She teaches us to focus on our objectives, to hold our head high, and to remain true to ourselves. Her lesson is one of boldness, of seizing every opportunity, and of going for our dreams.

GODDESS RITUAL

Reach your goal with confidence by performing this ritual to Skadi. Fill an ice mold with water, and add a couple of drops of lemon and orange juice to the mix. As you do this, think about your goal and see yourself achieving it. Imagine how it will feel and enjoy those emotions. Place the mold in the freezer, and when the liquid has turned into ice, remove and serve in a glass of chilled juice. As you sip say: "Skadi, goddess of winter's power, on this day, upon this hour, all my dreams I make come true, I stride forward in all I do."

GODDESS WISDOM

To break free from someone's influence and release his or her hold on you, use a little Skadi power. Write the name of the person on a piece of paper, place it in an ice bag with some water and leave in the freezer. Say: "I freeze your power and I let you go."

"Skadi, goddess of winter's power, on this day, upon this hour, all my dreams I make come true, I stride forward in all I do."

Chione

This beautiful Greek goddess of the snow has a sense of fun about her. Myths tell of her sitting in the heavens, looking down, and sprinkling her snowflakes upon Earth. A frivolous spirit, she was also a nymph and daughter of the mighty Boreas, the god of the north wind. In some tales, her mother is noted as Oreithyia, an Athenian princess whom Boreas kidnapped, but in others her mother is said to be the goddess of the chilly mountain winds. Either way, it was inevitable that Chione (or Khione) would govern snow, ice, and all things cold.

Her beauty and playful temperament ensured that she was sought after by many of the gods, but it was Poseidon who won her heart. She bore him a son, but was so afraid of how her father might react that she cast the child into the sea. Luckily, Poseidon was on hand to save the boy and transport him to safety. This might make Chione sound like a harsh and uncaring goddess, but, like the snow that she governs, she can go to extremes, changing from passionate and aggressive to light and gregarious in a heartbeat.

Her name in English means "Snow White." Related tales tell of another beautiful Greek maiden called Chione who had many admirers, including the gods Hermes and Apollo. However, this aspect of Chione does not fare so well. She becomes obsessed with her appearance and incredibly vain, comparing herself to the goddess Artemis. On hearing of her vanity, Artemis kills Chione by shooting her with a hunting arrow.

PLANET
Earth

STONE
Quartz, silver

FOOD / DRINK
Fresh water

FLOWER / PLANT
Any white flower—rose, lily, carnation

SCENT
Rose

ANIMAL TOTEM
Snowy owl

MISCELLANEOUS
Snow, wind, the colors white and silver

CHIONE

Chione is a goddess of two sides. A minor deity in the Greek Pantheon, she is still important, for she teaches us to embrace our frivolous nature. She encourages us to be spontaneous and have fun. Her lesson is one of joy, of searching for the light in every situation. She also urges us to be aware of the many different aspects of our personality.

GODDESS RITUAL

Attract more joy into your life with this fun ritual to Chione. Take a white or silvery scarf made of a light, see-through material. Wrap a piece of quartz in it and leave it sitting over night, while asking Chione to bestow her magical blessing. In the morning, remove the crystal and spray the scarf liberally with rosewater. Take it outside and hold it above your head while turning in circles to the left and right. Let the wind carry the scarf so it twists and dances. Finally, wrap it around your head and shoulders and say: "Like the snowflakes that fall, I embrace the dance of life!" Keep the quartz with you as a charm to attract happiness and good fortune.

GODDESS WISDOM
Even though it doesn't snow all year long, you can still tap into Chione's frivolous nature by embracing the fresh abrasive chill of the wind. Open all the windows in your home and let the breeze cleanse the space. Stand outside, arms outstretched, and imagine you're a flake of snow twisting and turning in the air.

"Like the snowflakes that fall, I embrace the dance of life!"

Angrboda

A potent weather deity and Norse ice goddess, Angrboda has the power to summon storms, ice, and snow. Her name means "foreboding," which fits with her fearless nature. Often thought of as a witch goddess, Angrboda is a powerful enchantress, and can appear in the form of a beautiful, golden-clad maiden or an old hag. She rules the iron wood, and is often called Hag of the Iron Wood since this is her preferred guise. A giantess created by the trickster god Loki, she bore him three evil children—Fenrir, the Wolf; Hel, the goddess of death; and Jormungand, the serpent that surrounds the world. The Norse gods feared Fenrir so much that they bound him with a magical chain, which was made up of the sound of a cat's footsteps, the beard of a woman, and the breath of a fish, among other magical items.

Despite Angrboda's scary reputation, she is also a mother goddess, and went on to have many more children whom she nurtured and protected, sometimes from the other deities. As the golden maiden, Angrboda is referred to as Gulveig, which means "power of gold," and shows a softer and more vulnerable side. Adept at shapeshifting, she often appears in the form of a crow and, in one legend, visits a childless queen to give her the apple of fertility. In this guise, Angrboda is associated with the cycles of life and death, while as the hag of the east wind, she would cause ships to sink or sail into trouble, just by singing to them.

A somewhat confusing deity, with many faces, Angrboda has an important lesson to teach. Despite terrible persecution at the hands

PLANET
Earth

STONE
Iron

FOOD / DRINK
Apple

FLOWER / PLANT
Trees of any kind

SCENT
Apple

ANIMAL TOTEM
Crow, wolf, snake

MISCELLANEOUS
Ice, frost, woods and forests,
the color gold, iron

of the gods, she still has the ability to love and nurture. She urges us not to judge a book by its cover, but to look deep into our hearts and find the good in others. Angrboda is not a victim—she rises up against adversity and challenges us to do the same.

GODDESS RITUAL

If you're facing a challenge, call on Angrboda with this easy ritual. Take an old iron key and bathe it in apple juice. Wipe it clean and find a quiet spot outside. Dig a small hole in the earth and bury the key. If you don't have a garden, use a plant pot inside—it will have the same effect. Place both hands on the soil you've laid on top and say: "Angrboda, come to me, help me with adversity. Help me rise above this pain. So that I may shine again."

Leave the key overnight. Remove it in the morning and keep it with you as a charm for bravery and strength.

GODDESS WISDOM

For some powerful Angrboda protection, wear something gold about your person. A piece of jewelry in the shape of a snake or a wolf is a great choice and will help you find the courage to face anything.

Death & the Underworld

The mysterious deities of death and the underworld are bountiful beings who will help you tap into your intuitive side and embrace life's ebb and flow. They know about the cycles of life, and the importance of light and dark. They shine with deep wisdom, and their knowledge knows no bounds. They understand that the secret to real happiness is in knowing yourself and embracing every aspect of your being. They will teach you how to face your fears and step forward into a new life. They will also help you to discover how to release any ties that are holding you back and emerge newly rejuvenated, ready to take on the world. Magic is their currency, and they will show you how to weave spells and manifest the things you want. Tap into their power through dreams and visualization. Let your imagination wander and let your subconscious speak to you and offer insights into an amazing future.

Persephone

PLANET
Venus

STONE
Amethyst

FOOD / DRINK
Pomegranate, honey, grain

FLOWER / PLANT
All flowering plants

SCENT
Lavender, vanilla

ANIMAL TOTEM
Bat

MISCELLANEOUS
Spring, meadows, flowers, the earth

This Greek goddess was the queen of the underworld, and married to the god Hades, although she had little choice in the matter. A beautiful spring deity, linked to fertility, new growth, and flowers, Persephone (Prosperina) was playing in the meadow one day with her nymphs when she was seized by Hades and carried to the underworld. Her mother, Demeter, searched high and low for her, and when she eventually found out the truth, she struck a deal   with Zeus, who had originally conspired to have Persephone kidnapped. Zeus agreed that the girl should be returned, but as she'd tasted the food of the underworld, in particular, some pomegranate seeds, she would have to remain in this realm for half of the year. The bounty of spring and the sudden flowering of all the meadows mark her return to the land of living every year. When she returns to the underworld, the seasons change, and the plants and flowers start to die as winter approaches.

Persephone is usually shown as a pretty young maiden, with flowers in her hair, holding sheaves of grain and a fiery torch, which lights her path in the underworld. Known for her compassionate spirit, Persephone was involved in many trials and tribulations, helping humans and gods alike. She lent Hercules the three-headed dog that guards the entrance to the underworld so that he could complete the challenge of the Twelve Labors. Youthful and innocent, this engaging deity won the hearts of many, including her husband's, and although she was dragged to the underworld against her will by Hades, she eventually fell for his charms.

Persephone teaches us that there is hope in every situation and light around every corner. Her lesson is one of trust and innocence, of having an open heart and a cheerful spirit.

GODDESS RITUAL

Attract a world of positive surprises and look to the future with optimism by performing this ritual to Persephone. Go outside, take a handful of mixed flower petals, and scatter them in a circle. Sit in the center of the circle, close your eyes, and imagine you're cushioned in the belly of the Earth. Feel the warm energy surround you. See a chink of light above, and imagine it raining down on you. Open your arms, stand up, and stretch as if you are a flower blossoming in the sunshine. Give thanks to Persephone for all of the blessings in your life.

GODDESS WISDOM

Introduce harmony into your home by creating some sweet floral displays for Persephone. Go for a bright mix of colors, including yellow, white, and pink, and lots of greenery. Supercharge your blooms by leaving a piece of amethyst near them.

Morrigan

This magical water goddess, whose name means phantom queen, governs death and destiny. Often appearing on the battlefield in the form of a crow or raven, she is associated with war and battles, and always seems to be present when souls pass over. She's thought to represent the cycle of life and death. A triple goddess, she has three forms—the Mother, the Maiden, and the Crone—and is most likely to appear as a wizened old hag, wearing a cloak of black feathers. Linked to the banshee, Morrigan is often seen washing the clothes of the dead in the river, or in her black bird form, perched on the shoulders of warriors who are about to die. This has given her a scary reputation, but the Celts revered her, believing her to be part of an ancient race called the Tuatha de Danann. To them, she had many roles, including Queen of the Faeries, and prophecy was one of her many magical gifts.

Not only does she lead souls to the afterlife, but she also guides magicians and sorcerers in their craft, acting as an intermediary between worlds, and often appearing as a hawk. She is present at magical initiations and called upon for her wisdom and protection. Thought to originate from an ancient cult called "the Mothers" or "the Disir," Morrigan is one of the most respected Celtic triple goddesses. Her connection to death means she is often worshipped at Samhain, more commonly known as Halloween.

If you have an interest in magic and the esoteric, you should be working with this goddess. Her message is one of regeneration,

PLANET
Moon

STONE
Obsidian, moonstone

FOOD / DRINK
Milk, oatcakes

FLOWER / PLANT
Mugwort, willow tree

SCENT
Clary sage

ANIMAL TOTEM
Crow, raven, hawk

MISCELLANEOUS
Rivers, streams, athame or dagger,
spear, crescent moon

of moving through the cycles of life, and of tapping into the power of each changing season. She teaches us to be strong, to weather the storm, and to stand up for our beliefs. She also urges us to follow our intuition and pay close attention to our dreams.

GODDESS RITUAL

To release your innate power, and improve magical abilities, use this Morrigan ritual. Take a piece of paper and either draw a large circle in the center or take the Wheel of Fortune card from a tarot pack and place it in the middle of the piece of paper. Focus on this image and imagine it's a Ferris wheel, and that you are sitting in the bottom carriage. Now feel the wheel turn and imagine you are rising to the top. Say: "As the cycle of life moves on, and the seasons start to spin, so the power of the Earth fills my soul within." Finish by asking Morrigan to bless you and give you a sign that you are on the right path.

GODDESS WISDOM

For protection and to promote prophetic dreams, add a few drops of clary sage to your bath water. Immerse yourself in the water and ask Morrigan to bless you with a vision of the future. You can also dab clary sage on a handkerchief and leave it on your pillow.

Kali

This powerful Hindu goddess has a dark side and is often linked to death. But rather than the physical manifestation of death, Kali is associated with the death of the ego. She tells us that we are more than flesh and blood, and that our spirit lives on, so death has no power over us.

An extremely compassionate goddess, Kali cares deeply about her followers. She is often pictured wearing a garland of skulls and a skirt made from dismembered arms, thus adding to her scary reputation. In reality, these items represent the physical body, and the liberation of her followers. She has four arms and hands. In one she carries a sword of protection, in another a demon's head. Her other two arms are free to protect and nurture the people. A fiercely protective mother goddess, Kali considers all humans to be her children. She is a creation goddess, and is believed to be the womb where all things were born, and where all things return, hence her link to the cycles of life. Often associated with burial grounds, because all worldly attachments are absolved in such places, many of her followers go to cemeteries to pray and give thanks for her blessing.

A goddess of new beginnings and endings, she is thought to govern the power of time. Her name comes from the Hindu word "kala," which means "time." She is often pictured with black skin, which represents her all-consuming nature. Although her appearance is terrifying, it is justified because it is Kali's way of keeping demons and any other evil entities at bay.

PLANET
Earth

STONE
Obsidian, smoky quartz

FOOD / DRINK
All fruits

FLOWER / PLANT
Jasmine, rose

SCENT
Sandalwood, jasmine, rose

ANIMAL TOTEM
None

MISCELLANEOUS
Cemetery, sword, the color black

Kali can help us cut the threads that tie us to the past. She can help us release those things that are no longer any good for us. We may be fearful about the future, but Kali is there to show us the way, and to keep our demons at bay. Her message is one of resurrection, of emerging into the light, and of overcoming fear.

GODDESS RITUAL

To cut any ties that are no longer beneficial, try this simple ritual to the goddess Kali. You will need to scoop up a cup of soil from a cemetery. Next (and you can do this bit at home) light a black candle to the goddess and sprinkle some of the soil in a circle around the candle. Take a few minutes to think about the tie you want to cut. Write on a piece of paper how you feel, and why you need to remove this from your life. Finally, take the paper and burn it in the flame. Gather up the ashes along with the remaining soil and sprinkle them outside. Say: "Kali, you have set me free, I move forward triumphantly!"

GODDESS WISDOM
Use Kali's power to help you face new challenges by keeping a piece of obsidian with you. Wear it close to your heart to keep you grounded and strong. In times of need, hold it in both hands, breathe deeply, and as you breathe out, imagine you're letting go of any negative thoughts that are holding you back.

Maat

PLANET
Venus, Jupiter

STONE
Clear quartz, lapis lazuli

FOOD / DRINK
Corn

FLOWER / PLANT
Lotus

SCENT
Lemongrass

ANIMAL TOTEM
Ostrich

MISCELLANEOUS
Ankh, feathers, outstretched wings

This stunning Egyptian goddess represents honesty, balance, and judgment. Her name means "truth" in Egyptian, and she was seen as the keeper of truth. Maat is often pictured seated, wearing an ostrich feather on her head and carrying a set of scales. She played an important role in Egyptian spirituality. Mistress of the dark, she was the one who weighed souls, standing at the gates to the otherworld with her set of trusty scales. It was her job to consider the fate of the soul, and to measure both good and bad deeds throughout a person's life. She did this with an ostrich feather, which was often referred to as the white feather of judgment and is sacred to the deity. She would weigh a person's heart and measure his or her true nature. If the heart weighed the same as the feather, the deceased would be allowed to pass on to the afterlife, but if the heart was heavy with bad deeds, that person would be devoured by the crocodile-headed god Ammut. Maat represented order in all things. She controlled the movement of the stars and the flooding of the River Nile every year, making her one of the most powerful and important Egyptian deities. The people looked to her for guidance and followed her rules in order to live a happy, prosperous, and peaceful life. She governed ancient customs and traditions, and encouraged the people to hold these close to their heart.

Maat shows us how to be true to ourselves. She urges us to consider the consequences of our actions, and to be honest and open at all times. Working with Maat will bring peace and harmony

to your life. One of her main lessons is that of balance and moderation in all things.

GODDESS RITUAL

To tap into Maat's powerful, rejuvenating energy, try this simple ritual. Gather together a handful of feathers of roughly the same shape and size. Tie them at the base with some white thread. Now use them like a feather duster to clean your aura. Use short flicking movements from the top of your head, down each side of your body to your feet, and imagine that you're flicking away negativity and stimulating the flow of energy. Say: "Goddess Maat, as light as feather. Cleanse my aura and my soul. Renew my life with light and vigour. Let happiness become my whole." You should feel energized and full of enthusiasm by the end of this ritual.

Freya

PLANET
Moon

STONE
Amber, ruby, citrine

FOOD / DRINK
Mint, berries

FLOWER / PLANT
Cypress, thyme

SCENT
Rose, sandalwood

ANIMAL TOTEM
Goose, cat, falcon

MISCELLANEOUS
Snow, wheel of fortune, flowers,
Friday (named after Freya)

This go-getting Norse goddess was known for her fighting spirit and winning charm. A warrior goddess, Freya was the leader of the Valkyries, a tribe of daring young women who made it their mission to collect the spirits of dead warriors and carry them to Valhalla. Only the bravest souls were picked, and it was Freya's job to help them make the transition into the otherworld.

One of her main roles was as a goddess of war and death. Often pictured wearing armor, or a cloak of feathers, Freya was believed to be the most beautiful woman in the world. An alluring enchantress, she could cast her spell over anyone just by flashing them a smile and letting them gaze into her eyes. She also had the help of a magical necklace of amber and rubies, which was crafted by dwarves. Called the Brisingamen, this stunning piece of jewelry was labeled "the necklace of desire" because it made the wearer irresistible. Freya, being a deity of love and beauty, had many admirers, but she did eventually settle down and marry the Norse god Od.

Tales tell of her riding through the sky in a gold chariot pulled by two enormous blue cats. These feline companions were a gift from the god Thor, who found them as kittens during a fishing trip to kill a sea dragon. He made a deal with the kittens' father, and took them back for Freya to nurture. Having such a big heart, Freya is fond of animals and is strongly associated with geese and falcons.

Sensual and charismatic, Freya teaches us to embrace our femininity and to make the most of our talents and strengths. Her

Freya.

lesson is one of love, appreciation, and seeing the good in others and ourselves. Work with her to increase your natural beauty and to radiate love.

GODDESS RITUAL

As well as her trusty necklace, Freya had a magical girdle, which intensified her natural beauty. Create your own super-belt to help you sizzle like a goddess. Take one of your favorite belts and leave it beneath the light of the full Moon. Invest in a piece of amber and place it on the belt buckle while chanting the following words: "Freya's allure is mine from this night, I let my natural beauty shine bright." In the morning, put the belt on, stand before a mirror, and repeat the chant while holding the amber in both hands. Keep the stone with you to increase your natural allure and attract good fortune.

GODDESS WISDOM

Improve your communication skills by chewing on fresh mint leaves. Alternatively, sucking a peppermint will have the same effect. Visualize your mouth clean and fresh and imagine that every word that falls from your lips is a sparkling jewel.

Oya

This magnificent African goddess had dominion over the natural world. Often called Bringer of Storms or Lady of Storms, she controlled the elements, including wind, rain, and hurricanes. If she felt like it, Oya could summon a cyclone or a storm from the gentlest breeze. A warrior queen with a fearsome nature, she was guardian of the underworld, the realm between life and death. This meant she could control the spirits of the dead. In some tales, she was able to raise them up or prevent them from passing over, depending on her mood. Oya is linked to cemeteries and funerals, and she is often worshipped in these places. She is also linked to spirit communication and clairvoyance. A goddess of witches, she is sometimes referred to as Great Mother of the Elders of the Night. This hints at her dark nature and her ability to see beyond the veil into the heart of all things.

A staunch protector of women she has a fiery nature, and works as both a nurturing mother and a terrifying opponent in battle. Oya represents the truth. To be dishonest goes against all her principles. Oya can sense deceit, and reacts by cutting it down. Like the storms that she governs, she is volatile and moody and is often thought of as a goddess of change, bringing new opportunities and closing doors to the past.

Her message is one of truth and honor. She urges us to be truthful in all things, including our innermost thoughts and feelings. Oya asks us to be fair, to look beyond the surface, and to trust our

PLANET
Earth

STONE
Garnet, carnelian

FOOD / DRINK
Shea butter, grapes, wine

FLOWER / PLANT
Cypress, yucca, eggplant

SCENT
Patchouli, geranium

ANIMAL TOTEM
Buffalo

MISCELLANEOUS
. Copper, coins, the colors red and purple, sword, wind chimes

gut instincts. If we are prepared to face the truth, she will help us move forward and create new opportunities for the future.

GODDESS RITUAL

If you want to turn your life around and attract new things and people, try this ritual to Oya. Remember that she's a powerful goddess who brings swift change, so be prepared for action. Take a jar and place it on your window ledge next to a purple candle. Drop a coin in the jar. Write down your wish on a piece of paper and drop that in there, too. Say: "Oya, almighty goddess of change, I welcome you into my world. I move forward with power and grace, from this moment, time, and place." Every day, light the candle, repeat the chant, and add a new coin to the jar.

GODDESS WISDOM

Embrace change and encourage new opportunities by celebrating the element of wind. Incorporate wind chimes into your home. If you prefer, dangle a selection of crystals from a piece of string by a window. Include some red-colored stones to please Oya.

*"Oya, almighty goddess of change,
I welcome you into my world.
I move forward with power and grace,
from this moment, time, and place."*

Lilith

Often called the Queen of the Night, or Dark Goddess, Lilith first appeared as a winged-bird goddess and wind spirit in Sumerian folklore. She had claws for feet and huge dark wings, and in some tales the lower part of her body was serpent-like. She has Babylonian roots and also appears much earlier in Hebrew myths and legends as the first wife of Adam. She is said to have left the garden of Eden because she would not comply with Adam's wishes.

A complicated deity with many associations, Lilith represents the female aspect of divinity. She is also a Moon goddess, and patroness of witches. Associated with the dark side of the Moon, and sometimes called a demon goddess, Lilith symbolizes the dark side of the soul, the nature that we try to repress. She is associated with childbirth and sexuality, and in Sumerian tales she was called Hand of Inanna because it was her role to take men from the streets and lead them to the temples of the sacred prostitutes. She lived in the sacred Huluppu tree, which was planted by the goddess Inanna. There she remained alongside a snake that could not be charmed and the Anzu bird and its young. The tree and its inhabitants were all untamed, adding to Lilith's reputation as being wild and mysterious.

Linked to prophecy, her animal companions are the owl and the snake or serpent. Lilith is portrayed as a powerful goddess, who is not afraid of her sexuality. She is proud of her exploits and of her true nature. Her message is one of innate confidence and strength.

PLANET
Moon

STONE
Obsidian, turquoise

FOOD / DRINK
Red wine

FLOWER / PLANT
Mandrake, vervain, mugwort

SCENT
Patchouli

ANIMAL TOTEM
Owl, snake, bird

MISCELLANEOUS
Feather, cauldron, black candles

She teaches us to be true to ourselves, to embrace both the dark and the light in our soul, and to face our fears. By accepting who we are, both the good and bad points, we can learn to be a better person.

GODDESS RITUAL

To connect with the goddess Lilith and to balance the light and dark in your life, make an altar in your living room. Cover a coffee table with a black tablecloth. Decorate the table with items associated with the goddess, for example, images of owls and snakes, feathers you have collected, a black candle, and a piece of obsidian or turquoise. Anoint the altar by burning some patchouli oil and lighting the candle. Make a wish to the goddess, and ask her to help you face your fears with renewed vigour and assurance.

GODDESS WISDOM

To improve inner strength and confidence, burn some patchouli oil and add it to a drop of sunflower oil. When you're feeling vulnerable, massage the mixture into your wrists, breathe deeply, and ask Lilith to bless you with her power.

Ceridwen

This powerful mother goddess is linked to the cycles of life and death. Keeper of the cauldron, and all forms of wisdom, Ceridwen had the ability to shapeshift and to conjure potent magic. She is best known for the tale in which she swallows her young assistant, Gwion Bach, because he mistakenly drinks drops of a potion meant for her own son. She chases after him in a number of guises, including a hare, an otter, and a hawk, until he eventually turns into a seed. Ceridwen transforms into a black hen and eats him. Gwion Bach is then reborn as the poet and bard Taliesin. The story represents a need to swallow the ego in order to be reborn and become free from the limitations of death. The message is that we all need to go through a series of changes, or small deaths, in order to reach our full potential.

Often associated with the dark side of the Moon and depicted as Crone, Ceridwen is considered the patron goddess of all witches. She has immense wisdom, but also the heart of a mother, making her approachable and nurturing, despite her connections with death and the underworld. She is associated with the harvest, and her cauldron contained a magical elixir of inspiration, the essence of the divine spirit. She would often appear to her people as a white sow, and because of this she was called the Sow Goddess or the Goddess of Transformation.

Since she gave birth to the famous poet Taliesin, she is thought of as the mother of poetry and often invoked for her creative talents.

PLANET
Moon

STONE
Agate, carnelian

FOOD / DRINK
Seeds, grains, nuts

FLOWER / PLANT
Vervain

SCENT
Bergamot

ANIMAL TOTEM
Crow, sow, otter, hawk

MISCELLANEOUS
Cauldron, hen, poetry

Her message is one of transformation. She urges us to grow and embrace change, to release all fear, and to move forward with optimism. Work with her to develop your creativity and to feel inspired and optimistic about the future.

GODDESS RITUAL

If you're looking for guidance or an insight into the future, ask for Ceridwen's help with this easy ritual. Take a small cauldron-shaped bowl and fill it with warm water. Sprinkle in a handful of seeds and some dried vervain, and add a couple of drops of lavender and bergamot essential oils. Stir the water and ask Ceridwen to guide you. Drain the liquid away, and you should be left with some of the vervain, arranged in a pattern. Spend a few moments looking at it, and see if any images or symbols spring to mind. Make a note of anything you see—it may be an insight into the future.

GODDESS WISDOM

Keep a creative journal and tap into your imagination. Dedicate it to Ceridwen, and ask her to inspire you by performing a mini-ritual. Light a white candle and burn some bergamot oil, place both hands on the book, close your eyes, and say: "By Ceridwen's light, upon this night, this book is blessed with my creative best!"

"By Ceridwen's light, upon this night, this book is blessed with my creative best!"

INDEX

ACKNOWLEDGMENTS

Thanks to all the folks at Cico books, and in particular Lauren Mulholland for her creative vision for this book, and her tremendous hard work at making it a reality.

Risa Palazzo for her amazing illustrations that really bring the deities to life.

And all those fabulous creative people that I work with regularly, who allow me to write about magic and folklore!

PICTURE CREDITS

Used under licence from *The Bridgeman Art Library,* 2013: p59 National Museum of India; pages 109, 115 Mucha Trust. Used under licence from *Corbis Images,* 2013: p16 Marc Dozier / Hemis; p21 Araldo de Luca; p28 Christie's Images; p32 Charles & Josette Lenars; p37 Werner Forman; p54 Fine Art Photographic Library; p66 Jason Horowitz; p72 Asian Art and Archaeology, Inc; p104 Images.com; p113 Hulton-Deutsch Collection; p126 David Cumming / Eye Ubiquitous; p132 Bettmann. Used under licence from *Getty Images,* 2013: pages 18, 80, 102 DEA Picture Library; pages 24, 49, 77, 96 DEA / G. Dagli Orti; p29 Spanish School; p34 Imagemore Co, Ltd; p40 UIG; pages 44, 128 Kenneth Garrett; p53 Mitza; p56 SSPL / Science Museum / Wellcome Trust; p71 Andrew Cooper; pages 83, 99 Time Life Pictures; p85 G Nimatallah; p88 Mondadori Portfolio / UIG; p106 Sir Edward Burne-Jones; p123 Henry Meynell Rheam; p139 John William Waterhouse. Used under licence from *Mary Evans Picture Library,* 2013: pages 62, 74, 133 Mary Evans Picture Library; p91 Sueddeutsche Zeitung Photo / Scherl. Used under licence from *Shutterstock,* 2013: pages 14, 42, 43, 68, 69, 94, 95, 118, 119.